WHAT PEOPLE ARE SAYING ABOUT

A Joy That Is Real

As a pastor, I'm always looking for fresh spiritual insight into Scripture and my good friend Dan Owens has once again hit a home run with his new book, A Joy That Is Real. *Dan has a user-friendly way of dissecting the book of Philippians and then uses life experiences to make the application. This is great as a devotional read for individuals, a study for Sunday school classes, or a resource for small groups discussion. This book is an encouragement to my life because it paints the biblical picture of how God wants us to live daily. We all need to know more about,* A Joy That Is Real.

DR. CLARK TANNER
BEAVERTON CHRISTIAN CHURCH, BEAVERTON, OREGON

In this new book, A Joy That Is Real, *Dan Owens outlines for us reasons to have joy. It seems we are all pretty good at convincing others we are happy, but Dan shows us that real joy is really attainable. Dan unravels Philippians in a way that exposes Paul to be that promoter of joy. Everyone wants to have joy, and Dan shows us how to be the people God designed us to be, while having joy.*

JERRY HUSON
PRESIDENT, SAN DIEGO CHRISTIAN COLLEGE

Dan has captured the wonderful balance of careful and accurate understanding with rich and practical application. The message of Philippians needs to be rehearsed again and again. Dan's book is a compelling guide.

BOB THOMAS JR.
SENIOR TEACHING PASTOR, CALVARY CHURCH, LOS GATOS, CALIFORNIA

Dan Owens has provided us with a look at the Philippian church in a way that provides needed personal application. It is easy to read a book about a portion of Scripture and walk away with new truths, yet fail to capture what those truths mean to us when we get up in the morning. This is not so with this book. Dan's probing questions and illustrations force us to engage with Paul's letter to the Philippians.

ALLEN QUIST
COAUTHOR OF *THE SPIRIT-DRIVEN CHURCH* (VICTOR, COOK
COMMUNICATIONS, 2006); ADJUNCT INSTRUCTOR, MULTNOMAH
BIBLICAL SEMINARY

Dan Owens' personalized and growth-focused approach is a balanced and practical help to any of us who find holding onto our joy a constant struggle. In writing about Paul's compassionate description of joy in the book of Philippians, Dan explains, "In all his writing he is so open, always letting us see straight into his heart." The same can be said of Dan's inspirational handling of this modern-day memento—the subject of joy.

DR. MARTY TRAMMELL
PROFESSOR OF ENGLISH AND COMMUNICATION,
CORBAN COLLEGE, SALEM, OREGON

A JOY
THAT IS REAL

A JOY
THAT IS REAL

DANIEL OWENS

Victor®

The Bible Teacher's Teacher

COOK COMMUNICATIONS MINISTRIES
Colorado Springs, Colorado • Paris, Ontario
KINGSWAY COMMUNICATIONS LTD
Eastbourne, England

Victor® is an imprint of
Cook Communications Ministries, Colorado Springs, Colorado 80918
Cook Communications, Paris, Ontario
Kingsway Communications, Eastbourne, England

A JOY THAT IS REAL
© 2005 by Daniel Owens

Published in association with the literary agency of Sanford
Communications, Inc., 6406 N.E. Pacific St., Portland, OR 97213.

The Web addresses (URLs) recommended throughout this book are
solely offered as a resource to the reader. The citation of these Web
sites does not in any way imply an endorsement on the part of the
author or the publisher, nor does the author or publisher vouch for
their content for the life of this book.

Cover Design: Two Moore Designs/Ray Moore
Cover Photo: iStockphoto 2006/Copyright: Allan Brown

First Printing, 2006
Printed in the United States of America

1 2 3 4 5 6 7 8 9 10   Printing/Year   11 10 09 08 07 06

ISBN-13: 978-0-7814-4187-2
ISBN-10: 0-7814-4187-0

LCCN: 2006927277

Gratefully dedicated to Dr. Floyd Roseberry who gave me the keys to unlock the cage of religion in which I had lived for so long. With his spiritual direction I have discovered life and joy in the Spirit instead of life in a theological system. As a pastor to pastors, a friend to the hurting, and a faithful counsel to those with questions, he has touched many lives through his long journey —but none more than mine.

CONTENTS

ACKNOWLEDGMENTS

I want to express my thanks to Craig Bubeck, who asked if I could write a book on the apostle Paul's letter to the Philippians. I was already halfway through the first draft—what a remarkable example of God's leading and providence! Craig's vision and encouragement have meant the world to me. I look forward to working together with Craig and his team on another book project in the near future.

My deep thanks to Carl Dawson, my "Barnabas" as we've served together with Eternity Minded Ministries around the globe. Your loyalty, tireless efforts, and joy in the Lord have been an inspiration to me.

Thanks to Karen Weitzel for typing the first draft of my manuscript—never an easy task! My deep thanks to David Sanford, president of Sanford Communications, Inc., who helped turn my publishing dreams into a reality. As well, special thanks to SCI associate editors Elizabeth Ries Jones and Elizabeth Honeycutt, who helped polish each chapter and added the application questions.

My prayer is that this book will bring a new depth of joy to many thousands of readers for God's glory, honor, and praise.

INTRODUCTION

A BOOK OF NOTHINGS

I t's been said that in any given church, 20 percent of the people do 80 percent of the work. This was *not* the case with the Philippian church, which Paul planted during his second missionary journey. Only a few years old, it is a noteworthy example of a young New Testament church. In part, this was thanks to Dr. Luke, who stayed behind when Paul moved on and who helped pastor the baby church during its first couple of years.

Not only had the church grown spiritually, but it was also growing numerically as well. From a small nucleus of believers— Lydia, the jailer and his family, a young woman who had been demon-possessed, and a few others—a full-fledged, thriving church developed. And they were active participants in Paul's ministry.

Thanks to their determined efforts to keep in touch with Paul and help support his missionary endeavors, Paul was still in close contact with the church in Philippi when he wrote this letter. He still knew all the old-timers by name and was still praying for them with deep, heartfelt concern.

As Paul pens this epistle, what is on his heart? What is on his mind? He's in a Roman prison for the sake of the gospel, but does he care? People are out in the streets preaching the gospel from false motives—slandering it, but does he care? Paul could be martyred for all he knows, but does he care?

I find it rather remarkable, in studying this epistle, to discover that Paul has *nothing* in mind when he writes to the Philippian believers. Several "nothings" in fact. These "nothings" spoke volumes to the Philippians and have much to say to us, as well. My prayer is that God will drive their message deep into our hearts and minds.

Let *Nothing* Terrify You

At the end of chapter 1, we read about the first "nothing." Paul, writing from prison, essentially says: "Whatever happens to me—whether I live or die—you keep right on living worthy of the gospel of Christ. How? Stand firm in one spirit, with one mind/soul striving together for the faith of the gospel. I know it isn't easy; Christ didn't call you to believe in him only, but also to suffer for his sake. You have adversaries aplenty. But, in *nothing*, no matter what they do, be terrified or alarmed by these opponents. Instead, remember their end (destruction) and stay true to Christ."

"In nothing be terrified or alarmed by your opponents." Is that true in our lives? Here is Paul, in prison, facing the possibility of death, unafraid and in fact being a witness for Christ in that dark, dreary place. What about us? Our circumstances are much different, of course. Our adversaries aren't quite so obvious, but they are just as real. In fact, our primary enemy, Satan, is the same then as now. "Be self-controlled and alert," Peter warns us. "Your enemy the devil prowls around like a roaring lion looking for someone to devour. Resist him, standing firm in the faith" (1 Peter 5:8–9).

Our adversary's first tactic to neutralize our witness and disrupt our Christian pilgrimage is to terrify and alarm us. If he can frighten us, then he's already won half the battle.

What has Satan done to frighten or terrify you lately? Paul would tell you, "Remember his end is destruction. Claim victory in Christ as you run to him—your rock, fortress, and hiding place."

Do *Nothing* Out of Selfishness

Paul goes on to talk about a second "nothing" in Philippians 2:2–3. Once we've dealt with our adversaries, we need to look at our relationships with one another as part of the body of Christ meeting together. Paul says in effect: "Make me happy by being of the same mind, maintaining the same love, united in spirit, intent on one purpose." How is that possible? The secret is in chapter 2, verse 3. "Do *nothing* out of selfish ambition or vain conceit (selfish nothingness), but in *humility* consider others *better* than yourselves."

As if that isn't clear enough, Paul reemphasizes his point in verse 4. He wants us to take special note of this. He says, "Each of you should look not only to your own interests, but also to the interests of others."

Paul says this is the key to enjoying *oneness* of mind, spirit, and purpose. When people observe how we interact and relate to one another in the church and outside, they should say, "These people really do care about others." And that, of course, is the key to our witness before a watching world. "By this all men will know that you are my disciples," Jesus said, "if you love one another" (John 13:35).

Christ Made Himself *Nothing*

How is it possible to do nothing from selfish motives? Let's look at the third "nothing," in chapter 2, verses 5–7. There Paul says, "Your attitude should be the same as that of Christ Jesus: Who, being in very nature God, did not consider equality with God something to be grasped, but made himself *nothing*." Think of it: God, the Creator and master and sovereign of the universe, stepped off his throne in heaven and humbled himself. He became invisible—nothing—taking the form of a commoner, of a bond-servant, the lowest of low among mere men.

Not only that, but Christ humbled himself by obeying God, the Creator, in the face of horrible adversity, to the point of death—execution, capital punishment, crucifixion on a cross. Imagine! The God of glory became the scum of the earth. Except for the generosity of someone who finally spoke out for Christ, his body would have been tossed away like filth to rot. Of course, we know the end of the story. God the Father raised Christ from the dead and exalted his name. One day everyone, even the devil himself, will bow down and acknowledge that Christ is Lord, to the glory of God the Father.

But if Jesus Christ could do that for us, lowering himself from heaven, making himself *nothing* when he is truly *everything*, can we not lay aside our natural selfishness and love each other in obedience to Christ? Thanks to his work in our hearts, yes!

Don't Work for *Nothing*

If you do that, Paul says in Philippians 2:14–16, what a witness you'll be to this crooked and perverse generation. You'll appear as children of God, as shining stars in the universe, holding out the word of life. If that's true, Paul tells the Philippian believers in verse 16, "I'll know I haven't worked, labored, or toiled for *nothing* in this life. Even if I'm martyred, it will have been worth it all."

Have you ever stopped to think of everything that people have invested into your life as a Christian? Not only to see you come to Christ, which for some of us wasn't an easy task, but also nurturing you in the faith, teaching you the spiritual ABCs as best they could; introducing you to the Bible, to prayer, and to the importance of meeting together as brothers and sisters in Christ—to the basics.

I don't think anyone wants to take those things for granted. Some of the people who have invested in our lives have already gone on to be with the Lord. Yet, their sacrifice and service is still bearing fruit as we keep the faith. Let's hold fast, walking blamelessly in love, hand-in-hand before a watching world.

Everything Else Is Less than *Nothing*

In chapter 3, Paul talks about what might prompt someone to throw away their faith, to the disappointment of those who have invested in their lives. When you look at the alternatives to faith in Jesus Christ, however, Paul says they're *less than nothing*, worthless, rubbish, dung. Consider the world's man-made religions and cults. At best, Paul says in chapter 3, verses 7–8, they're a complete *loss* when compared to the *surpassing greatness* of knowing Christ Jesus our Lord.

In fact, Paul says, knowing Christ is so great that it isn't something we can fully attain in this life. But as we identify with his sufferings and death, and experience the power of his resurrection, we're getting closer to the prize—the reward that God has called us to in Christ.

Have you discovered the surpassing value of knowing Christ Jesus yet? Do you know him as your Lord? If so, press forward to know him even better. Toss out anything in your life—whatever it is—that may be hindering you from knowing Christ better. Is there unresolved conflict in your life? As far as possible, settle the matter. Is there unconfessed sin? Admit it to God and be rid of it. Are you hanging on to some area of your life when God is saying "let go"? Count it as *nothing*—toss it away—so you can know Christ better.

Transforming the Body of *Nothing*-ness

In chapter 3, verses 16–21, Paul speaks of a sixth "nothing" that directly relates to the importance of knowing Jesus Christ.

First, in verse 16, Paul urges us to keep living up to the degree of Christian maturity we've already obtained. He doesn't want us to fall back into the old patterns of sin. Instead, he says in verse 17, imitate those who walk in a godly manner.

But whatever you do, avoid those who have turned against Jesus Christ, who have proven to be enemies of his cross. Paul gives this warning with tears flowing down his cheeks. These were people he thought would turn to Christ. Instead, they have rejected Christ. To these people, the humiliation of Christ on the cross is scorned. They hate what it represents. Why? Because it is directly contrary to their own selfish, conceited ways. They'll have nothing to do with a God who would let himself be hung and who commands us to makes ourselves *nothing* so we can serve others too. As Paul notes, the end of such haters of the cross, whose god is their own belly, is sure destruction.

In contrast, our citizenship is in heaven, and we eagerly wait for our Savior, the Lord Jesus Christ, who will transform the *body of humiliation*, the body of nothingness we now inhabit (a body of humiliation like that which God himself inhabited for thirty-three years). He will fit us with a body like his own resurrected body of glory, by his tremendous power that created and sustains the universe. One day we will no longer be "nobodies," but princes and princesses, co-regents of the King of kings.

Worry about *Nothing*

Paul speaks of one more "nothing," and with this prepares to close his letter to the Philippian believers. Look at chapter 4, verses 6–7, for a minute. "Be anxious for *nothing*, but in *everything* by prayer and supplication, with thanksgiving, let your requests be made known to God" (NKJV). When we do this, the peace of God that surpasses all comprehension will guard our hearts and minds in Christ Jesus.

Whatever your situation today, Paul says, take your concerns to the Lord in prayer. Are you feeling the attacks of the evil one? Then pray. Are you struggling to keep regarding others as more important than yourself? Tell the Lord that, too. Do you want a more Christlike, servant attitude? Tell God.

In the midst of personal struggle or outward trials, don't worry about anything, Paul says. Not by denying reality, but by taking it all to the Lord—and then trusting him that he's still in control. He understands how we feel and will gladly give us his supernatural peace, which will stabilize us in the midst of the toughest storms.

We find that the book of Philippians is really about nothing and everything at the same time. As we dive into our study together, I trust you will discover many new truths that will help you to grow in joy through our Lord.

CHAPTER 1

LET THE JOY BEGIN

PAUL AND TIMOTHY, SERVANTS OF CHRIST JESUS, TO ALL THE SAINTS IN CHRIST JESUS AT PHILIPPI, TOGETHER WITH THE OVERSEERS AND DEACONS: GRACE AND PEACE TO YOU FROM GOD OUR FATHER AND THE LORD JESUS CHRIST. I THANK MY GOD EVERY TIME I REMEMBER YOU. IN ALL MY PRAYERS FOR ALL OF YOU, I ALWAYS PRAY WITH JOY BECAUSE OF YOUR PARTNERSHIP IN THE GOSPEL FROM THE FIRST DAY UNTIL NOW, BEING CONFIDENT OF THIS, THAT HE WHO BEGAN A GOOD WORK IN YOU WILL CARRY IT ON TO COMPLETION UNTIL THE DAY OF CHRIST JESUS.

—PHILIPPIANS 1:1–6

The apostle Paul tends to intimidate even the most mature believers. It's hard to relate to a man who is a Christian superhero. Paul seemed to do everything excellently. He was an incredible orator, statesman, theologian, and missionary. How could we even hope to measure up to the life of Paul?

The book of Philippians gives us a good look into the apostle's life and heart. The book is not just a theologian's textbook. Paul gives us the opportunity to see what his life is really like. Through examining Paul's life, we begin to see what made this man tick—the Lord Jesus Christ.

Paul chose to live his life joyfully. He tells the Corinthian church, "I have great confidence in you; I take great pride in you. I am greatly encouraged; in all our troubles my joy knows no bounds" (2 Cor. 7:4). Despite his troubles, and Paul certainly had plenty of them, he was able to say, "My joy knows no bounds."

In studying Philippians, it is important to remember that Paul wrote this short epistle while in prison. He had been illegally arrested, beaten, and put in chains. It's hard to tell by his attitude, though! While he could easily have thought, *Life isn't fair,* he chose to have joy. We all have times when life doesn't seem fair or seems especially cruel. How do you respond in those times? Paul was in bad shape. Yet this trial was not a source of bitterness for him but gave him reason to rejoice.

In Roman times, there were a couple different ways to be imprisoned. One was under house arrest in which the prisoner was chained in his own home where he awaited his trial. The other way was to actually be put in prison, in a dungeon twelve feet under the ground, where the prisoner would wait to be executed.

Although Paul ended up experiencing both kinds of imprisonment, at this time he was under house arrest. People could come and see him, but his living situation was quite unpleasant.

I've had the opportunity to travel to various places around the world and minister in quite a few prisons. I don't know how those people deal with it. The prisons in the United States are certainly not places you would like to spend a weekend in, but compared to prisons in the rest of the world, ours are wonderful. One prison in Northern Ireland, which was in operation as recently as 2000, was called the Maze. The prisoners there had a five-foot by five-foot cell with no light; they got one bowl of soup a day. I don't understand how they survived from year to year.

A Romanian pastor spent a lot of time in prison because he believed in Jesus. He wrote, "It was amazing how you could see Jesus shine in the face of other believers, even in a Communist prison. We did not wash. I had not washed for three years, but the glory of God shone even from behind the crusted dirt."

He went on to say that after his release, people would look at him and wonder what was different about his life. He wrote,

"They could not understand my joy in suffering because they could not think beyond the difficulties of their own life: an abusive husband, a nagging wife, or troublesome children. But these material difficulties and tempests in your soul, how can they compare to the joy of knowing Jesus?"

This man had spent a lot of time in prison; he had been beaten and starved almost to the point of death, yet the reality of knowing Jesus Christ was something that came alive to him. He said, "All the things of the world, all the things that people think are so important—compared to knowing Jesus as my Savior—they just kind of fade away."[1] Paul writes from prison. He writes with joy. You may wonder, "Is that really possible?"

Joy in Greeting

Don't overlook the joy in Paul's greeting in verse 2. He begins the letter to the Philippians by saying, "Grace and peace to you." In Paul's time, letters generally included a health wish. Today, we would say, "I hope this letter finds you well." Paul's greeting does not merely wish good health on his readers. He is blessing the Philippian church with a "Christian health wish."

"*Grace … to you.*" Paul's relationship with this church had its origins in God's grace. Not favoritism that would be earned; this is grace—what God gives to those who do not deserve it. Even Paul, the early church's Superman, finds his reason for living and his ability to minister solely in God's grace.

"*… and peace.*" The grace that we have in Jesus leads us to peace. The word for peace in Greek is *eirene*. The corresponding Hebrew word is *shalom*, meaning wellness or wholeness. By giving this blessing, Paul reminds the Philippian church of the result of grace in a believer's life: peace.

The word *peace* has several meanings in the Bible. It can mean peace with God, signifying that an individual has made peace with God through Jesus Christ. Peace can also refer to our inner emotions. Are you at peace internally? As you experience peace with God, you will find peace with yourself because you know that your sin is forgiven.

A third meaning refers to peace within a believing community. Paul often deals with this in his letters. Even in the Philippian church, as we'll see later in the book, a couple of women were not getting along and were in desperate need of this type of peace. Finally, peace can mean peace in worship, in coming together and communing with God. Inner peace comes from having peace with God. Once we have that inner peace, our community of peace should grow as well.

Which peace is Paul referring to in verse 2? Although it is not clear, it is possible that he is referring to the first three: peace with God, inner peace for the individual, and peace within their community. This peace springs from knowing God's grace and experiencing it yourself. The Bible says, "You will keep in perfect peace him … [who] trusts in you" (Isa. 26:3).

Joy in Memories

In verse 3, Paul writes, "I thank my God every time I remember you." The Philippian church, in the time between then and his imprisonment, had given Paul reason to thank God when he thought of them.

We also know that the Philippian church gave more money to the apostle Paul than any other church. They weren't a rich church—they weren't rich people—but they gave more money to his ministry than anyone else, and there was affection because of that.

One time, after I spoke to a small mining community outside of Charleston, West Virginia, the people there came to me and handed me a check made out to Eternity Minded Ministries for six thousand dollars. It was a tiny community with very little money, but they wanted to give to our ministry to share the good news with people around the world.

As I thought about them, I remembered the Philippian church, and I understood Paul's feeling of connection with these people. They were saying to him, "We know you need the money. You are sharing the gospel and we want to be a part of that." They prayed for Paul, they sent people to help him, and they gave to him financially. They had a partnership. Paul was joyful; the gospel was moving forward because of their help.

At the time Paul wrote Philippians, he was in a desperate situation—locked up in chains, forced to obey commands without knowing what the outcome was going to be or what would happen to his life. Yet as he thought back over his memories of the Philippian church, he was content and joyful in the midst of his suffering.

Joy in Prayers

We get a glimpse of Paul's prayer life in verse 4. "In all my prayers for all of you, I always pray with joy." Paul isn't just spouting off some glib phrase. He doesn't say, "I'm thinking about you all the time." That wouldn't be honest. However, he does say that he thanks God every time he thinks of the Philippians and he prays for them with joy.

Paul begins his letter to the Romans in a similar way. He writes, "First, I thank my God through Jesus Christ for all of you, because your faith is being reported all over the world. God, whom I serve with my whole heart in preaching the gospel of his Son, is my witness how constantly I remember you in my prayers at all times; and I pray that now at last by God's will the way may be opened for me to come to you" (Rom. 1:8–11).

We can safely assume that Paul had an awesome prayer life. One of the reasons for that, I believe, is that he allowed his prayers to be guided by the Holy Spirit. Do you ever have times when, out of nowhere, somebody comes to your mind? You weren't thinking about the person before, you may not have seen him or her for weeks, or you may have no contact whatsoever. All of a sudden, a face flashes into your head. What do you do?

Paul is saying, "Every time I think of you, every time you come to my mind, I pray for you." In the middle of the night, you wake up and a face, a name, comes across your mind. What for? I believe the Spirit of God brings people to our minds to pray for them at just the right time. When we follow God's prompting and follow through in praying for that particular person or situation, we are walking in the Spirit and learning to "hear his voice."

I once read a biography of Hudson Taylor, the great missionary who started China Inland Mission. One night his mother woke up in the middle of the night and felt led to start praying for her son, who was hundreds of miles away. She hadn't had any contact with him for quite some time, but at that very moment, Hudson was deciding whether or not he would follow Jesus. His mother just kept praying, although she didn't know why at the time. Later she found out that at the same time the Lord brought him to her mind, Hudson was making the biggest decision of his life.[2]

As you go through the week and people come to your mind, even if you don't know what's going on in their lives, consider that the Lord may be prompting you to give someone a phone call, or write a note of encouragement, or just stop and pray for someone.

In verse 5, Paul mentions his partnership with the Philippians, "Your partnership in the gospel from the first day until now." The Greek word is *koinonia*, meaning fellowship, a two-sided relationship. They had something in common—the gospel! Sharing God's grace, the message of Jesus Christ, was their common ground.

Joy in Expectations

Paul was expecting God to do a lot in the lives of the Philippians. "Good works" in verse 6 refers to the transformation of their Christian life, which had given them this spirit of generosity. The Philippian church had learned something very important about the kingdom of heaven—that joy does not come in getting what we want, but by letting go of what we don't need. They knew what they needed and what they didn't need, and they gave generously to Paul. Paul's expectations were not so much on the people as they were on God. He was saying, "I can hardly wait to see what God is going to do in your life" while trusting God to complete that work of transformation in their lives.

Sometimes we look at our own lives and think, *I'm not feeling too transformed right now.* Maybe we doubt that God is really working in our lives. Too often we try to produce transformation in our own lives or in the lives of those around us. We forget that it is really God who does the transforming. We can partner in that transformation by praying for others and by allowing him to change our hearts.

As Paul looked at the Philippian church, his confidence was not in the Philippians. His confidence was in God. God, who began a good work in these people, was going to complete it (1:6).

As you reflect on your own life, perhaps you are ready to hand the transforming process over to God. Or maybe God has brought someone to your mind this week whom you need to pray for. You may want to send a "health wish note" in order to be an encouragement to this person.

Paul was no Superman, though we sometimes put him in that category. He was real. He was human. He had problems. He had struggles. That will come out more as we continue our study. It's nice to know we're in good company as we make our way through the book of Philippians.

CHAPTER 2

A PRAYER FOR GROWING LOVE

*IT IS RIGHT FOR ME TO FEEL THIS WAY ABOUT ALL OF YOU, SINCE I
HAVE YOU IN MY HEART; FOR WHETHER I AM IN CHAINS OR
DEFENDING AND CONFIRMING THE GOSPEL, ALL OF YOU SHARE IN
GOD'S GRACE WITH ME. GOD CAN TESTIFY HOW I LONG FOR ALL
OF YOU WITH THE AFFECTION OF CHRIST JESUS.*

*AND THIS IS MY PRAYER: THAT YOUR LOVE MAY ABOUND MORE
AND MORE IN KNOWLEDGE AND DEPTH OF INSIGHT, SO THAT YOU
MAY BE ABLE TO DISCERN WHAT IS BEST AND MAY BE PURE AND
BLAMELESS UNTIL THE DAY OF CHRIST, FILLED WITH THE FRUIT OF
RIGHTEOUSNESS THAT COMES THROUGH JESUS CHRIST—TO THE
GLORY AND PRAISE OF GOD.*

—PHILIPPIANS 1:7–11

I recently received an e-mail from a friend who has been walking with the Lord for many years. He confessed to me that he still does not sense the love of God in his life. As I thought about his situation, I realized that he did not have the growing love that Paul prays for in this passage.

Paul loved these people dearly. His desire was to see growth among his people, the people he led to the Lord in the church he planted. They have shared in God's grace with him (v. 7), and his affection for them leads him to pray this beautiful prayer.

Eugene Peterson paraphrases it this way in *The Message: The Bible in Contemporary Language*. "So this is my prayer: that your love will flourish and that you will not only love much but well. Learn to love appropriately. You need to use your head and test your feelings so that your love is sincere and intelligent, not sentimental gush. Live a lover's life, circumspect and exemplary, a life Jesus will be proud of: bountiful in fruits from the soul, making Jesus Christ attractive to all, getting everyone involved in the glory and praise of God" (Phil. 1:9–11). Let's look at a few aspects of this growing love.

The Nature of Growing Love

My son Taylor is a pretty happy kid who enjoys life. But I wonder how his life and emotional state would be different if people around him started telling him things like, "Your dad doesn't really love you. In fact, he doesn't want to be around you very much. Did you know that you really irritate your dad all the time?" Sadly, in some families this is reality, and I know the damage it does.

What would your mindset be like if someone told you those kinds of things about your father or about your mother? What would your perspective be toward your parents? Sometimes in our experience, unfortunately sometimes even in church, we get it into our heads that God is really not for us. We think that he is disgusted with us and out to get us. We end up with a warped idea of how God truly feels about us.

As I read the e-mail from my friend, I spotted this problem. How could this man have a growing love when he's not even convinced that God loves him? Without that understanding, it's impossible to love someone else the way we should. As Alexander MacLaren said, "No man loveth God except the man who has first learned that God loves him."

In this passage, Paul uses the Greek word *agape* for love. He's referring to the love that is a divine love. The one great distinction between *agape* and *phileo*, or brotherly love, is that he is speaking not of a reciprocal love but a self-sacrificing love. This love is not tied to an object. It is love for the sake of love, self-sacrificing love, and a love without the promise of anything in return. It's the kind of love that only the Holy Spirit can put into our hearts.

As humans, we don't often have this *agape* love because we always want something in return. "I love you; you love me back. I give something to you; you give something back." Too often we use the physical world to determine our love for something. I look at a motorcycle, and I can tell you whether or not I love it. We look at people and oftentimes determine whether or not we love them by their outward appearance.

The apostle Paul is saying, "That's not the kind of love Christ wants to grow in our hearts." Jesus uses the example of the Good Samaritan in Luke 10 when he tells us what kind of love we should have. The story starts off with an expert of the law asking Jesus, "Who is my neighbor?" He was looking to detach himself from any kind of responsibility. Jesus never answers the question directly, but instead tells the story, then asks him, "Which one was a neighbor?"

The follower of Jesus knows no boundaries of love. But if we don't believe that God loves us or that he likes to "hang out" with us, how can we express that kind of love to someone else? Paul prays that our love will abound, growing more and more. That is the work of the Holy Spirit.

Mike Yaconelli, in his book *Messy Spirituality*, tells the story of a young college student who went on a short-term mission trip to an inner city neighborhood. He walked up to a dilapidated tenement building and knocked on one of the doors. An African American woman, smoking a cigarette and holding a crying baby on her hip, opened the door. He asked if he could share a little about Jesus Christ with her, and she proceeded to give him a string of expletives and slammed the door in his face.

Quite discouraged, the young man walked away and sat down on a curb. Suddenly he had an idea. He remember that the baby hadn't been wearing a diaper, so he walked down to the corner store and bought some diapers and a pack of cigarettes and went back to the woman's house. This time he asked if he could come in and give her the items and help out. He spent the entire afternoon cleaning, taking care of the baby, and talking with the woman. By the end, she asked him to pray for her.[1]

Sharing Jesus isn't just about preaching. I enjoy doing large evangelistic crusades, but I also cherish the times that we spend in refugee camps and in the communities doing relief work. Growing love involves sacrificing time, money, and comfort in order to reach out to those who need to hear our good news.

The Environment for Growing Love

The New Testament has two Greek words generally translated "knowledge." One refers to knowledge for the sake of intellectual pursuit—knowledge that you gain from reading, from studying, from observing. The other kind of knowledge is knowledge that you get from actually experiencing the situation or event.

It is interesting to note that Paul uses the word that means knowledge by experience when he prays that "your love may abound more and more in knowledge and depth of insight." We have to experience God.

As I walked into the associate pastor's office at a Presbyterian church, the first thing I noticed was all of his diplomas. He had one from Cal Poly, and one from a prestigious seminary on the East Coast that was all in Latin. I thought, *Those are nice looking diplomas.* He mentioned that he was working on another diploma at the time, one from Fuller Theological Seminary.

He explained that at the East Coast seminary, everything was about intellect, ivy towers, and books. He was going to Fuller to really learn how to do ministry. "The seminary looked good, but they didn't teach me how to deal with hurting people or people who are demon possessed," he said. This pastor was describing intellectual knowledge versus experiential knowledge. Do you truly experience God, or do you just have a lot of book learning?

I once read the story of Father Damien, who ran a ministry to a leper colony in Hawaii in the 1800s. At that time there was no cure for leprosy, and it was a horrible way to die. Father Damien felt that the Lord had put it on his heart to go work with the lepers there on the island of Molokai.

After several years of working with the lepers and not seeing any fruit, Father Damien made the decision to touch the people. Although he knew he was signing his own death warrant, he realized that they were never going to accept him and understand the love of Christ until he touched them, because in their culture, touch was the way to convey meaning and love. Without touch, just standing there and saying "I love you" did not mean anything.

At the same time, there were Puritan missionaries on the Hawaiian Islands who would come and preach to the leper colony. However, they would not touch these people, and they preached down to them. So when they spoke about the love of God, the people didn't have a clue what they were talking about. Father Damien made himself one of the lepers, just as Jesus showed, and he eventually contracted leprosy and died.

If you visit Hawaii, you will see many statues of King Kamehameha, whom the native islanders revere, but you will also see a statue of Father Damien. To the people, he is a man who truly loved them and experienced life with them.

Paul prays for the Philippians to have a growing love in the environment of experiential knowledge. The result, he says, is that they may be able to discern what is best, and be pure and blameless until the day of Christ. A growing love fed by proper knowledge and moral insight enables us to see the best way to live in light of our standing with Christ.

The Need for Growing Love

In relationships, the longer you are with a person, the more you need this Christlike love. When you're dating, you are always on your best behavior; you always put your best foot forward. So when my wife and I do premarital counseling, we always ask, "Have you fought yet?" If they say, "Oh, no, we don't fight," then we know they are in trouble. You have to know that this person you're about to marry is different, that he or she won't always agree with you. If you only ever see the best side, you are in for a big shock!

The longer you're in a relationship, the more your love for that other person should continue to grow. Unfortunately, many couples have separated because they are shaken when life changes and reality sets in. They don't realize that marriage takes three parts: intimacy, passion, and commitment. All too often they leave off the third part entirely.

For a short time we attended a certain church in San Diego. Each Sunday morning, people would walk in, sing the songs, listen to the message, and walk out. They did not visit with each other, and nobody wanted to be involved in ministries or leadership. They just wanted to go to church and be happy. The only problem is, life is messy. You and I are messy. It is our commitment to love one another that allows us to overlook the faults of others.

Many of us think that "love" and "yes" go together. But that is not necessarily true. We tell our kids, "No, you can't do that." Why? Because we love them. God also says "no" at times, because he loves us too much. Love may be confrontational and tell someone, "We care about you. You're on a path of self-destruction." That's where discernment is needed. Paul points out in verse 10 that our goal is to be able to discern what is right.

Sometimes that might mean saying "no" to something that is good. You could serve on this committee, and run that program, and keep yourself so busy that you can't get fifteen or twenty minutes alone with the Lord. Paul is saying, "I'm praying that your love will grow so that you will discern not what is important and what is unimportant, but what is *best.*"

Paul's prayer is that our love may grow and abound continually, because you can never have too much love! In our culture, we tend to attach our love to objects, but God wants us to have a love for other people that gives unconditionally—without expecting anything in return.

CHAPTER 3

JOY IN JAIL!

NOW I WANT YOU TO KNOW, BROTHERS, THAT WHAT HAS HAPPENED TO ME HAS REALLY SERVED TO ADVANCE THE GOSPEL. AS A RESULT, IT HAS BECOME CLEAR THROUGHOUT THE WHOLE PALACE GUARD AND TO EVERYONE ELSE THAT I AM IN CHAINS FOR CHRIST. BECAUSE OF MY CHAINS, MOST OF THE BROTHERS IN THE LORD HAVE BEEN ENCOURAGED TO SPEAK THE WORD OF GOD MORE COURAGEOUSLY AND FEARLESSLY.

—PHILIPPIANS 1:12–14

In some ways, Paul was like a mass evangelist—he wanted to reach the multitudes. Paul had wanted to go to Rome for a long time, because he knew that if he could win the city, he'd win the masses. In a place of great influence like Rome, he could impact many people with the gospel.

But instead of going to Rome as a preacher, Paul went as a prisoner. He wasn't really expecting that. In Acts 21, you can read about the riots, Paul's illegal arrest, being in prison for a couple of years in Caesarea, his appeal to Caesar, the threats on his life, his trip to Rome, the shipwreck, the house arrest, his restricted freedom, and his upcoming trial—all these hardships that eventually landed him in prison.

To the regular person, Paul's situation might seem pretty bad, but God was at work and using the situation for his glory, as Paul points out in verse 12. And Paul was joyful through it all. He was joyful in his situation because he knew that God had a plan.

Joyful in His Environment

Paul wanted to put his readers at ease. They were waiting with bated breath to find out if he was going to be condemned or acquitted. For the Christians, this was a distraction. Paul was a famous leader. What was going to happen to him?

Paul explained that all these things happened to him for a reason. He says, "Now I want you to know, brothers, that what has happened to me has really served to advance the gospel." What a great word: *advance*. It's a military term that means to go ahead of the troops and prepare the way. Paul is using that same word, *advance*, meaning "going ahead."

The Philippians were afraid because their leader, the one they looked to, was locked up in prison. It seemed like it was all over. From a human perspective, it would have been easy to consider Paul's situation and say, "What's going to happen to the message of the gospel? What's going to happen to these churches because one of our leaders is incarcerated? What are we going to do?"

Paul could have sat in prison thinking, "What is happening to me? This is a terrible situation. I've got all these things to do." Instead Paul was thinking in a completely different way.

Paul lived in a different realm that we, too, can live in. He had a different worldview—not of his world, but God's world. In a way, the advances of the modern world we live in—education, technology, industrialization—are our greatest threats. Our "advances" have stolen from us the very thing that made the early church so effective. Our "advances" have stolen away our true belief in the supernatural, reducing life to this material world that we live in—what we can taste, what we can see, what we can touch, what we can smell. Paul understood that life is not all about this material world that we live in—it goes much farther than that. It is beyond that. It is actually a spirit world.

If you were in Paul's situation, you would probably be pretty disappointed and depressed. But Paul, looking through his worldview and knowing how God works, saw it as an opportunity for the gospel to move forward. To him, the most important thing was not his physical comfort; it was that the saving message of transformation was being proclaimed.

Joyful in Evangelism

Paul took advantage of his environment to share the message of Christ. Even though he was in chains twenty-four hours a day, he wasn't chained to a wall. He was chained to another person. Every four to six hours, around the clock, a new soldier would come in and have to sit with Paul. Can you imagine those poor guards to whom he was chained? I'm sure Paul took advantage of every opportunity to talk their ears off!

From a human perspective, we might think that God could have accomplished more through Paul if he had not been in prison. But if Paul had been left alone to teach in synagogues, I don't think his influence would have been as great on Rome's political leaders. Because he spent day and night chained to a member of the emperor's own elite troops, he was able to share Christ with some very influential people.

As Americans, we are kind of programmed to think that life should be a certain way. We are concerned about our education, our home, our cars, our job, our spouse and kids, and if we don't have that, we view life as a tragic failure. We don't see that God might be at work in our difficult circumstances.

When I was twenty-three years old, I went through a desert stage of life. Maybe you have been there too. Dry, barren, depressing, unfulfilled—a life desert. At the time, I was newly married, working for a furniture store, and struggling to earn enough money. I made brass furniture, and I came home every night covered with black stuff, filthy dirty, and tired.

It took me a while to realize it, but God was working in

me. And not only was God working in me, he was working through me.

I began to realize that I had quite an opportunity to share Christ with two people at work, Jack and Gail. We shared many lunch breaks where we would sit outside and talk. Jack was a real thinker, and we would dive into many subjects, often turning to spiritual things. It was an incredible opportunity that I would not have had if I'd continued to go through my days feeling sorry for myself and my situation.

Even in the desert, even in the dark times, even when things look bleak, remember that the Lord has placed you in your particular circumstances for a reason. If you have a worldview that sees through the tough times and recognizes the opportunity to advance the gospel, like Paul did, God will bless your efforts.

In Matthew 28, when Jesus gives the Great Commission to his disciples, he uses the Greek word *poreuthentes* in a structure that should literally be translated "as you are going." You don't have to be a foreign missionary to fulfill Christ's command. Paul shared the gospel right where he was, and so can we.

I wonder how many of us have really thought about advancing the gospel where we work, where we shop, where we live—with the people we see every day. We know that the gospel always has ripple effects. One person comes to the Lord and then someone else comes to the Lord because of him or her. Christianity has always grown that way. I pray that we have that kind of courage and boldness to seize every opportunity to advance the gospel, as Paul did.

Joyful in His Encouragement

When the other believers found out that Paul was in prison, they had two choices: They could either stand with him, or they could go into hiding. Paul made a point to joyfully encourage them.

When I was a student in Mr. Jackson's seventh-grade history class, I learned an important lesson about the two choices the Philippians faced. One day we were out on the playground discussing Mr. Jackson's class and how boring it was. Some of us decided that something needed to be done, and somehow I got suckered into being the spokesperson. It was probably that red-headed girl who got me into it! Besides, all the kids were telling me they would back me up if I would be the first to tell Mr. Jackson how we felt.

So the next day in class, as Mr. Jackson stood up to teach, I raised my hand and began to let him know how we felt about his class. Amazingly, when I started speaking it seemed like everybody in the room just kind of disappeared and it was just Mr. Jackson and me. All my friends who had promised to stand by me just stared silently. I learned something very important that day: When the heat is on, most people run. I also realized that I really hurt Mr. Jackson. Even to this day, I can see the look on his face as I humiliated him in front of his class.

The heat was on for the Philippian Christians; Paul was probably wondering what they were going to do. Would the church go underground? Would they run and hide? Actually, Paul says, "Because of my chains most of the brothers in the Lord have been encouraged to speak the word of God more courageously and fearlessly."

The word *speak* does not refer to preaching but everyday conversation. These Christians were encouraged to continue speaking fearlessly, courageously for Jesus in their everyday interaction with people.

Our enemy is real, and he wants us to stop talking, stop sharing, become discouraged and defeated, and ultimately to give up. It doesn't matter if you're in prison, like Paul was, or if you're the CEO of a large company. We need to remember where the real battle is—the spiritual battle—and seize every opportunity to preach Christ.

CHAPTER 4

WHY ARE WE HERE?

NOW I WANT YOU TO KNOW, BROTHERS, THAT WHAT HAS HAPPENED TO ME HAS REALLY SERVED TO ADVANCE THE GOSPEL. AS A RESULT, IT HAS BECOME CLEAR THROUGHOUT THE WHOLE PALACE GUARD AND TO EVERYONE ELSE THAT I AM IN CHAINS FOR CHRIST. BECAUSE OF MY CHAINS, MOST OF THE BROTHERS IN THE LORD HAVE BEEN ENCOURAGED TO SPEAK THE WORD OF GOD MORE COURAGEOUSLY AND FEARLESSLY.

IT IS TRUE THAT SOME PREACH CHRIST OUT OF ENVY AND RIVALRY, BUT OTHERS OUT OF GOODWILL. THE LATTER DO SO IN LOVE, KNOWING I AM PUT HERE FOR THE DEFENSE OF THE GOSPEL. THE FORMER PREACH CHRIST OUT OF SELFISH AMBITION, NOT SINCERELY, SUPPOSING THAT THEY CAN STIR UP TROUBLE FOR ME WHILE I AM IN CHAINS. BUT WHAT DOES IT MATTER? THE IMPORTANT THING IS THAT IN EVERY WAY, WHETHER FROM FALSE MOTIVES OR TRUE, CHRIST IS PREACHED. AND BECAUSE OF THIS I REJOICE. YES, AND I WILL CONTINUE TO REJOICE.

—PHILIPPIANS 1:12–18

I can only imagine what it will be like in heaven to worship the Lord in his presence. I can't wait!

While we are here on earth, though, we should be doing three things as joyful Christians who live out our faith in power and love. First, we should worship the Lord. Second, we should grow together with other Christian believers. And third, we should tell others the good news of Jesus Christ.

Worship. Grow. Tell. That's the three-fold mission of the church. And we find it here in this passage.

Do you ever find it hard to worship the Lord? Or grow together with other believers? Or tell others about the good news of Jesus Christ?

Many believers struggle with the third aspect of our mission—witnessing. Maybe it's fear, maybe it's laziness—but we often have a hard time stepping out of our comfort zone and bringing the good news of the gospel to our friends and family.

The apostle Paul didn't let fear or laziness deter him. In fact, he kept right on witnessing despite myriad unfortunate circumstances. Things were certainly not going as he planned. First of all, he was imprisoned. Later we learn that his friend Epaphroditus had been seriously ill, and that Paul must also part with his beloved friend Timothy. In the midst of these trials, Paul is able to say, "I rejoice." Why? Because Christ was being proclaimed.

Ross's Story

A friend of mine, David Sanford, had a unique and unexpected encounter shortly after September 11, 2001. He tells the story best:

> I left work a couple minutes early that day to make sure there was no way I could miss the #89 express bus. My mind was already racing ahead to that evening's youth group parents meeting at my church.
>
> After I stood at the bus stop for fifteen minutes, it became clear that the bus wasn't on schedule.

Twenty-five more minutes rolled by. No express bus. I couldn't believe it. This was messing up everything. Forget eating dinner with my family; I'd barely get to church on time. Finally, the 5:35 p.m. #89 rolled into view. Who knows what happened to the 4:55 p.m. bus.

So far, things were not going the way I had planned. Trying to keep up a good attitude, I stepped aboard, took a seat, and pulled out my Bible to get focused for the parents meeting.

Just then, a nineteen-year-old young man interrupted my quiet time. "What are you reading?" he asked.

Oh, great, I thought. *Just what I need, another disruption to my already messed up schedule.* However, I smiled and replied, "The Bible."

"How come?"

"Well, I try to read the Bible each day," I said.

"That's cool." The inquisitive young man smiled. He was dressed in a green Nike T-shirt, camouflage pants, a backward-facing baseball cap, with a three-day-old stubble. "You know, I like reading the Bible too. My favorite part is Ecclesiasticals."

"Oh?" I replied, with a slight smile on my face over his interesting pronunciation.

At that point, my friend—Ross, I learned later— went into a brilliant, almost ten-minute exposition of the central themes of Ecclesiastes, quoting several passages almost verbatim. I was impressed! And I could tell many of our fellow passengers were listening in on our conversation. Inwardly, I laughed. *This guy must be a Multnomah Bible College sophomore in disguise.*

"Wow, that's amazing," I told Ross. "You're right: That's what that book is all about. What other books of the Bible have you read so far?"

"Well, Revelation—and Matthew, Mark, Luke, and John."

Ross then explained that he had realized eternity is the most important question we need to settle in this life, preferably while we're still young. "I was an atheist all the way through school," he confided. "After high school, though, I didn't want to go to college. Instead, I signed up to serve my country. My gig is guarding the Portland International Airport," Ross said. "See these fatigues? I'm wearing a big fat sign that says, 'Shoot me first,' if a terrorist ever attacks the airport."

Ross ranted a bit about America's weaknesses, then picked up on a couple of the themes in Ecclesiastes, weaving in his interpretations of Revelation. "I don't understand it all, but I'm convinced all this bad stuff is going to happen—probably in my lifetime." Ross glanced out the window again. I still hadn't figured him out—*pretty eclectic,* I thought.

"You know," Ross continued, "I went to church as a boy, but I don't have much use for it. I never understood this stuff back then. Besides, the church has too checkered of a past. They've forgotten what Jesus was all about. You know, he was the perfect Son of God. He never hurt anyone. He never hated anyone. Instead, he died on the cross for our sins. He's changed my life. Not that I'm perfect; no one is." He pondered that last point, gazing out the window again.

"I think it's important to accept everyone the way they are," Ross continued. "I keep trying to explain all this to my old girlfriend—we're still friends, even though she's in Wicca. She keeps reminding me of the bad things the church did to witches in the past. That wasn't right."

"No, that wasn't right," I agreed.

My stop had come into view, so I reluctantly ended our conversation. I thanked Ross for sharing with me.

Twenty-five minutes later I arrived at church—late
for the parents meeting. I started the meeting by
commenting that unexpected things sometimes happen. And then I told Ross's story.[1]

My friend David's encounter with Ross illustrates what it
means to advance the gospel in the midst of everyday life and
circumstances, even those that we don't expect or plan.

Our Motivation

When unexpected things happen in your life, what's your
first response? Do you get frustrated and annoyed? Are you
tempted to be angry? Or is your first priority to tell other people
about the good news of Jesus Christ? That's exactly what the
apostle Paul wanted to do! Not that he enjoyed all the hard
things that happened in his life. But he transformed those trials. He changed them. He converted them from something bad
to something good.

In verse 12, Paul points out that his circumstance—that is,
his house arrest—was serving to advance the gospel. Think
about it: Paul was able to witness to everyone who came to his
home, whether they came with pure motives or not. He could
talk about the good news of Jesus Christ with each of the soldiers who were forced to come to his home and keep him under
lock and key. Then, those soldiers and others who visited Paul
turned around and repeated what he said to other people. Also,
Paul had plenty of time to send a prolific amount of correspon-
dence to Philemon and to the churches in Ephesus, Philippi,
Colossae, and other cities.

Let's not forget that Paul had written a powerful sixteen-
chapter letter to the Romans before this visit. He probably had
it recopied many times while he was under house arrest. That
immensely important letter and Paul's personal testimony were
a powerful one-two punch. In addition, many scholars believe

it was during this house arrest that Dr. Luke collaborated with Paul and wrote the book of Acts.

In other words, we can account for the writing of about eighty-five pages of the Bible during this two-year window of time. And every one of those writings focuses on and repeatedly talks about the good news of Jesus Christ—the gospel message that brings salvation.

I like what Ross said: "They've forgotten what Jesus was all about. He was the perfect Son of God. He never hurt anyone. He never hated anyone. Instead, he died on the cross for our sins. He's changed my life." And he wasn't afraid of telling others. In fact, he was quite bold!

What does it take to be bold for Jesus Christ? In verse 14 Paul uses two words to describe it: *courageously* and *fearlessly*.

The terms *courage*, *courageous*, and *courageously* appear thirty-five times in Scripture. Seven of those times, Joshua and the people of Israel are exhorted to be courageous as they prepare to enter the Promised Land. Several other times Jesus exhorted his disciples to take courage; and then a few years later Jesus appeared to Paul and told him the same thing.

In turn, Paul repeatedly urged others to take courage— because of God's sure promises and because of the need for action. People need the Lord. As my friend Luis Palau says, "We've got to tell them that God wants everyone to go to heaven. That's good news!" Jesus wants them happily worshipping, growing, and telling still others. God has a plan for their lives.

Not only is God's Word proclaimed courageously, but it is also proclaimed *fearlessly*. Some 365 times Scripture talks about being *fearless*, *without fear*, or *not afraid*. Why so many times? Because fear is a natural human response to troubling circumstances.

So how do we respond fearlessly to life's troubles? First, by remembering what God's Word affirms to be true about God himself and about our future. Our future is settled; it's guaranteed. There's no need to fear. The worst thing that could happen to you and me is nothing compared to the goodness waiting for us in God's presence. And the reality is, God is already present within us. If we've placed our faith in Jesus Christ, God's Holy Spirit already indwells us. He's our guarantee that God will keep his promises. Therefore, we can trust God and not give in to fear.

We respond without fear by remembering what our purpose is, which is to worship the Lord, grow together with other believers, and tell other people about the good news of Jesus Christ. We can move forward in obedience to God with holy boldness, not fear, no matter what our circumstances.

The next time you are running late or your day has been turned upside down by unforeseen issues, stop and think: Is God trying to get my attention? Does he want me to be a witness right where I am, even if it's not in the place where I intended to be?

On a trip to Uganda, several things did not go as we had planned. When our team first landed in Entebbe, we learned that we would need an armed escort from the State Department in order to travel safely to Lira, four hours north. A rebel force known as the Lord's Resistance Army had been threatening people in the area. Consequently, we were required to hire armed security. The threat of these rebels was so great that our driver who was supposed to take us to Lira ran away and we had to find someone else.

When we finally reached our destination, we discovered that the local engineer who had been hired to run the sound system had also run away. Although we didn't know it at the time, God had already provided for that need through a guy on the ministry team who came with us. This man actually ran sound for a living at a community theater, and he easily stepped into the role.

Despite these obstacles, God provided for us every step of the way, and around seventy thousand people participated in the events during the four-day evangelistic festival. Approximately five thousand adults and children committed their lives to Jesus

Christ. The circumstances may not have happened the way we planned, but they were never out of God's control, and he worked everything out for his glory.

Although Paul didn't plan on being under house arrest, he had the confidence that he was there for a purpose. He knew, as he wrote in Romans 8:28, "that in all things God works for the good of those who love him, who have been called according to his purpose."

Is there anything that can stop you and me from worshipping, growing, and telling? Unexpected circumstances, troubles, or trials? No. House arrest? No. Death itself? Again, the answer is no.

Oswald Chambers said, "When the darkness of dismay comes, endure until it is over, because out of it will come that following of Jesus which is an unspeakable joy."[2]

CHAPTER 5

JOYFUL CONFIDENCE

FOR I KNOW THAT THROUGH YOUR PRAYERS AND THE HELP GIVEN BY THE SPIRIT OF JESUS CHRIST, WHAT HAS HAPPENED TO ME WILL TURN OUT FOR MY DELIVERANCE. I EAGERLY EXPECT AND HOPE THAT I WILL IN NO WAY BE ASHAMED, BUT WILL HAVE SUFFICIENT COURAGE SO THAT NOW AS ALWAYS CHRIST WILL BE EXALTED IN MY BODY, WHETHER BY LIFE OR BY DEATH.

—PHILIPPIANS 1:19–20

Someone has said, "Confidence is that quiet assured feeling you get just before you fall flat on your face." I'm not sure that is quite right. Paul wasn't always confident in every aspect of his life, but in the things that mattered, he was quite confident.

Paul's confidence was not in himself—it was in the Lord. He knew that even from jail he could still have the joy and strength of the Lord, because God was in control even in bad situations.

In this passage, we read about several things that gave Paul confidence that can also give us confidence today.

Confidence of the Holy Spirit's Ministry

Back when Paul was writing this book, they didn't have telephones or computers. You might wonder: What did they do for a prayer chain? Prayer chains are a marvelous ministry. You can call one person—"This is the problem; would you pray?"—and that person calls the next person and so on until everyone is praying. I don't think that a day goes by where I don't receive something reminding me to pray for someone.

Even without a prayer chain, Paul tells the Philippians that their prayers are helping him. Paul couldn't pick up the phone and say, "Hey, church at Philippi, would you pray for me in this situation?" A letter would take months to reach them. Paul had to depend on the ministry of the Holy Spirit in prayer.

Scholars agree that the "Spirit of Jesus Christ" in verse 19 refers to the Holy Spirit, the Comforter whom Jesus promised to send. Paul knew that when things got really difficult, the ministry of the Holy Spirit in his life was going to be very important. He was on trial for his life, but he had confidence in the strength that was going to come from the prayers of other people and the ministry of the Holy Spirit in his life.

I believe that one of the ministries of the Holy Spirit is to make us aware that someone else needs prayer. The Lord may bring people to your mind for you to pray for when you're driving down the street, or when you're at work, or wherever you might be.

Paul is saying to the Philippians, "Because of your prayers, because the Holy Spirit has reminded you to pray for me, I am going to be able to do what God has called me to do in this situation." The prayers of other people are so important.

Do you sense the ministry of the Holy Spirit in your life bringing you comfort, bringing you encouragement, bringing you joy in situations that most people would not see as joyful?

Scott Bauer, the pastor of The Church On The Way in Van Nuys, California, had a wonderful ministry. He was a great communicator and his congregation loved him. Scott was preaching one Wednesday night when he got an extreme headache. He had an aneurysm and by Friday night, at the age of forty-five, Scott went to be with Jesus.

How will those people cope with the loss of their pastor, their shepherd? From our vantage point, there are no answers, but they cope with the comfort of the Holy Spirit. Paul knew that. He knew that God was in control but that he was going to need to be comforted by the Holy Spirit.

My son Ben plays the guitar. I am continually amazed by how he can play without any sheet music. As I wondered how he learned to play so well, I remembered a dark time in his life.

During his freshman and sophomore years of high school, right after we had moved from Portland, Oregon, to San Diego, California, he sat in his bedroom for hours and hours practicing those scales over and over again. The move had been rather upsetting to him, so he turned to guitar to release his emotions. Now he plays with the worship band. God used a difficult time of his life and brought something good out of it.

Paul knew that even in his imprisonment, something good was going to come of it through the Philippians' prayers and the comfort of the Holy Spirit.

In Romans 15:30, Paul wrote, "I urge you, brothers, by our Lord Jesus Christ and by the love of the Spirit, to join me in my struggle by praying to God for me." I love that phrase, "the love of the Spirit." God loves you. The indwelling Holy Spirit loves you and is ready to minister to you according to your need. The Holy Spirit produces in the believer an immediate and overflowing consciousness that he or she is the object of God's love.

People will tell me, "I don't feel like God loves me." The first thought that comes to my mind is, *Have you really experienced being filled with the Holy Spirit?* Because God says that his Spirit is a Spirit of love. Paul uses the words "the love of the Spirit." In Romans 5:5 Paul writes, "And hope does not disappoint us, because God has poured out his love into our hearts by the Holy Spirit, whom he has given us."

I love to read the story in Acts 19 of Paul's visit to Ephesus. Some disciples there had not even heard of the Holy Spirit, but when Paul began to tell them, a transformation took place in their lives.

Sometimes I think Christians feel the same way. "We know about God. We know about Jesus. But we're not sure about this Holy Spirit." The Holy Spirit is called the "Comforter." And his work is so important in our lives. The Holy Spirit unifies us to Christ. The Holy Spirit ties my spirit to his Spirit; he gives us comfort when no one else can give comfort.

Confidence of Courageous Manners

Verse 20 says, "I eagerly expect and hope that I will in no way be ashamed, but will have sufficient courage." Paul wanted to stay on course. He knew that God had something for him; and he knew that his beliefs were being tested by fire.

So much of what we say we believe has yet to be tested. When we lose a loved one, we're faced with the question: What do I really believe? When we get an ailment, a physical infirmity that comes out of nowhere, we have to wonder: Is what I believe really true?

One time, before I got up to speak at an evangelistic event in Southern California, I heard a man give an incredible testimony. He had been raised in a Christian home, gone to church and to a Christian school, but he had become a drug addict. His parents' faith didn't really have a great impact on his life.

As he continued to share, we learned that he was now the pastor of a church. So what happened? Somewhere along the line he realized that it had to be his own faith. He couldn't just say, "I believe." His life was tested and he came to a point where he understood what being a Christian was really about.

"Pray that I'll stand firm. Pray that I will be courageous in what I do," Paul says. Do you ever pray for boldness? One of the great evidences of the Spirit's work in our lives is courage. Timid creatures and self-absorbed individuals become different when the Spirit transforms their lives. He gives us that courage, that power to change. Paul wanted to have this courageous manner about him.

When I was a youth pastor many years ago, we took a group of high school kids to summer camp at Hume Lake. One of them was seventeen-year-old Alan, who came with a friend from our youth group. Alan decided to accept Christ that week.

I had lost track of Alan, but recently we came across his family and they invited us over for dinner. He's an optometrist now, with a wife and kids, and he's serving the Lord faithfully. After camp that summer, Alan came home and shared Christ with his brother, who eventually became a missionary to Africa. Their mom also came to the Lord. I was amazed at the power of the Spirit to transform a life.

As we talked, Alan shared with me that he had been diagnosed with multiple sclerosis. I couldn't believe it—here was this big, healthy guy who worked out, had a wonderful family, and now he was facing this sickness. But he wasn't rattled. He told me of all the ways God had led him through the years. "I'm in God's hands," he said. "He knows what he's doing." That is a man with courageous manners.

Confidence of Christ's Magnification

Why did Paul want this courage? He says in verse 20, "so that now as always Christ will be exalted in my body, whether by life or by death." Paul understood that God's kingdom was the most important issue at hand. He saw the big picture. He knew that God wanted him to magnify Christ through his life.

One day at the airport I picked up a magazine called *Mysteries of Outer Space*. In it was a picture taken by the Hubble telescope. The object of the picture was twelve billion light years away. It was just a little slice of the universe—fifteen hundred galaxies. Now remember, in our galaxy, the Milky Way, it would take one hundred thousand years to get from one end to the other, traveling at the speed of light—approximately 186 thousand miles per second. Yet, fifteen hundred such galaxies were picked up in one photo from the Hubble telescope.

What does a telescope do? It reaches out and brings objects that are far away into view. It has incredible power to bring distant things into focus.

What Paul was saying here is, "I want to magnify Jesus. I want to bring Christ into view for people who cannot see clearly, who do not understand. Whether I'm alive on planet earth or whether I die, I want my life to be used as a telescope to bring Christ closer to people." That was his goal. That was his driving passion.

Judy was a woman whose life truly exemplified Paul's prayer that "Christ will be exalted in my body, whether by life or by death." She was active in our church and had a wonderful family and a healthy life. Within a short period of time, her husband died and she was diagnosed with multiple sclerosis. The disease slowly crippled her to the point that she couldn't move any part of her body except her head. She was confined to a wheelchair that she pushed with a button in her mouth.

Despite these circumstances, Judy never stopped smiling. She came to church every week, even though it was quite a chore. Her joyful, radiant smile greeted me each week, and I never once heard her complain about her condition. She continued to serve and encourage wherever she could. Christ was certainly magnified to me through her life.

In 1 Corinthians 6:20, Paul instructs believers to use their bodies for God's glory and honor. Our lives should guide others toward salvation. Do you magnify Jesus in your life? We have everything we need in order to have joyful confidence and courage in knowing Christ!

CHAPTER 6

MOVING FROM JOY TO JOY

FOR TO ME, TO LIVE IS CHRIST AND TO DIE IS GAIN. IF I AM TO GO ON LIVING IN THE BODY, THIS WILL MEAN FRUITFUL LABOR FOR ME. YET WHAT SHALL I CHOOSE? I DO NOT KNOW! I AM TORN BETWEEN THE TWO: I DESIRE TO DEPART AND BE WITH CHRIST, WHICH IS BETTER BY FAR; BUT IT IS MORE NECESSARY FOR YOU THAT I REMAIN IN THE BODY. CONVINCED OF THIS, I KNOW THAT I WILL REMAIN, AND I WILL CONTINUE WITH ALL OF YOU FOR YOUR PROGRESS AND JOY IN THE FAITH, SO THAT THROUGH MY BEING WITH YOU AGAIN YOUR JOY IN CHRIST JESUS WILL OVERFLOW ON ACCOUNT OF ME.

WHATEVER HAPPENS, CONDUCT YOURSELVES IN A MATTER WORTHY OF THE GOSPEL OF CHRIST. THEN, WHETHER I COME AND SEE YOU OR ONLY HEAR ABOUT YOU IN MY ABSENCE, I WILL KNOW THAT YOU STAND FIRM IN ONE SPIRIT, CONTENDING AS ONE MAN FOR THE FAITH OF THE GOSPEL WITHOUT BEING FRIGHTENED IN ANY WAY BY THOSE WHO OPPOSE YOU. THIS IS A SIGN TO THEM THAT THEY WILL BE DESTROYED, BUT THAT YOU WILL BE SAVED—AND THAT BY GOD. FOR IT HAS BEEN GRANTED TO YOU ON BEHALF OF CHRIST NOT ONLY TO BELIEVE ON HIM, BUT ALSO TO SUFFER FOR HIM, SINCE YOU ARE GOING THROUGH THE SAME STRUGGLE YOU SAW I HAD, AND NOW HEAR THAT I STILL HAVE.

—PHILIPPIANS 1:21–30

Generally speaking, people don't look forward to dying. Most of us will do anything to keep from dying, and few of us choose to think or talk about death. But the apostle Paul had some great thoughts on death.

"For to me, to live is Christ and to die is gain," Paul says in verse 21. I have to be honest with you. That passage has always bothered me a little bit, because I don't always feel that way. It is an incredible statement. To die is even better than being here on earth. It sounds good and spiritual. It sounds like true commitment to the Lord, but I don't always feel that way.

I know what Paul is saying and I know that what he is saying is true. It's just that I don't always feel that way. I look at Paul and think, *He didn't have a family—he didn't have a wife and kids.* So for Paul to say "to live is Christ and to die is gain" is not the same as my saying that. I certainly don't go through every day thinking, *Yeah, for me to live is Christ but, man, I'd rather check out and go to heaven and be with God.*

How many guys have you known who have excitedly joined the military right out of high school or during college? They are young and gung ho and ready to fight. Then, somewhere along the way, they meet a wonderful woman, and soon they marry and have a family. Suddenly, the thought of dying isn't quite the same. They have to think of the family back home while they are off fighting.

When I read this passage, I realize that it is a good thing to aspire to, but honestly, I'm not always there. Maybe I'm weak, maybe I'm immature, or maybe I'm not a very strong Christian. I tell God, "Lord, I love you, but leaving my wife and my children is not something that I really want to do right now."

The truth is that most of us would really rather stay alive than die if we have the choice. God understands that. In Ecclesiastes 2:24–25, Solomon recommends, "A man can do nothing better than to eat and drink and find satisfaction in his work. This too, I see, is from the hand of God, for without him, who can eat or find enjoyment?"

Paul certainly enjoyed life, but he had a bigger picture. He had joy in his present circumstances, and even more joy in his future circumstances.

Knowing Joy Now

A lot of us would feel as Paul said, "I am torn between the two." The wonderful thing is that you and I don't have to make that choice. Our lives are in God's hands. God has ordained our days. He knows the number of our days on planet earth, whether we're going to go home to be with him at forty-seven or seventy-seven or a hundred and seven. We are going to enjoy heaven. But right now, we can also enjoy this life. We can enjoy Christ right now.

I'll never forget a man in Lavita telling me, "Dan, you're always talking about Jesus in the future. We're going to go see him. Well, will you tell us about enjoying him right now?"

We *can* enjoy him right now. We can enjoy the strength of Christ that gives us the ability to endure and to become people we would not be otherwise. We can enjoy the mind of Christ that allows us to see life completely differently from other people. We can have the humility of Christ that says, "God is everything. We worship him alone and we direct all of our praise to him, just as Jesus did."

We have the experience of Christ. We experience him in our communion, our union with him. We experience his presence with us on a daily basis. We can rest in Christ knowing that he is working through us and in us. We have the comfort of Christ, knowing that whatever happens in our lives, we are truly in his hands and he has not made a mistake with us.

We also have the power of Christ, the power to impact other people's lives, the power to do the things that he's asked us to do, the power to fight off the schemes of the enemy.

I pray that you are enjoying Christ right now. "For to me, to live is Christ." Maybe because he wasn't so tied to this earth Paul was able to say, "I'd rather go and be in heaven, but as long as I'm here, it's about Jesus."

Experiencing Joy Later

Paul truly did have the desire to die. It was not a suicidal thought. It was not due to depression. It wasn't because he was having such tremendous physical pain that he wanted to be released from his body. No, it was the thought: *I'm enjoying Jesus so much right now. How much more fully am I going to enjoy him in heaven?* In Paul's heart he knew the ultimate joy was to be with the Lord.

For Paul, the whole issue is intimacy. That's what he was looking for and talking about. Why? *Because the closer I am to death, the closer I am to being with him forever.*

After my wife, Deb, and I were first engaged, we lived far apart. We spent a lot of time writing letters back and forth and making phone calls. That was okay, but it wasn't the same as being in each other's presence. We wanted that intimacy.

Paul is saying, "There's going to come a time when death is gain because it brings more of Christ to me and more of me to Christ." That is something that he truly looked forward to. That was the final destination.

The word Paul uses in verse 22, "body," actually means "flesh." He is reminding the Philippians that this body is just flesh, a soul cage, filled with weakness and disease. These bodies of ours are going to let us down at some point.

I was reminded of this recently when we learned that a friend of ours has contracted a disease for which there is no cure. This disease causes all the tissue in the body to harden, whether it is skin tissue or vital organs. The hardening can't be stopped, and over time she will lose all flexibility in her muscles, and then the disease will spread and begin to harden the tissue of her heart, liver, and lungs.

As I thought about this friend, I realized that as wonderful as these bodies of ours are, they can really throw us a curve ball. We can die from so many different diseases, and we don't know when our time will be up.

Paul had hope because he knew what was in store for him. In 2 Corinthians 5:1–2 he says, "Now we know that if the earthly tent we live in is destroyed, we have a building from God, an eternal house in heaven, not built by human hands. Meanwhile we groan, longing to be clothed with our heavenly dwelling."

In the 1990s movie *Flatliners*, five medical students had this great idea to die and bring each other back. In other words, they killed one person at a time and then would resuscitate him, letting him go as far as he could on the other side and then come back. It made for a great science-fiction movie, but the whole point was about wondering what is on the other side.

For those of us who know Jesus, we know what's on the other side. Yes, we lose loved ones and the pain is incredible. However, we have the great confidence of knowing that we are going to be with them forever! If there were no thought, no hope, no reality of heaven, what a depressing world this would be. We have the confidence of knowing that we will experience the joy of Christ more fully someday.

Being a Source of Joy

What was it that enabled Paul to move from "I would like to go to heaven now," to "I think it's better if I stay here for you"?

Life and death held a certain attraction to Paul. He was torn between the two. Paul truly had the mindset that loving God was the most important thing in the world, and after that came service to other people.

A pastor friend of mine shared an inspiring story with me that beautifully illustrates this mindset. Kearney was talking with his wife one day when she told him about a conversation she overheard at the store. One of the ladies working there had a four-hundred-dollar car bill, and she was upset because she didn't know where she would get the money to pay it.

The next day Kearney was praying, and he felt the Spirit of God tugging at his heart. He called the store and asked around until he found the woman with the car repair bill. He explained to her that his wife had overheard her talking about the situation, and that God was prompting him and he wanted to help her out.

This woman, Rachel, started weeping. She had followed Christ at one point, but had walked away from him. Now, out of nowhere, she had a phone call from a man she didn't even know who wanted to pay her bill. Kearney and his wife have spent time with her and she's coming back to the Lord.

I've heard that a wise church leader once said, "God has three sorts of servants in the world. Some are slaves and serve him from fear. Others are hirelings and serve for wages. The last are sons and daughters who serve because they love."

Perhaps you have discovered that truth. You love God, you love Jesus, you're filled with the Spirit, and you want to serve. You serve other people and your life is meaningful. It doesn't matter what your qualifications are. Your life is meaningful because you're motivated out of love and you serve out of love.

Maybe you haven't discovered it yet. You think that life and joy is all about you, about people meeting your needs, listening to you and taking care of you. I pray that you will discover the truth that joy comes from serving other people.

Paul understood this very well. While he was on this earth, he wanted his life to be used by God to serve others. Someone once said to me, "There are two ways to walk into a room. You can walk into the room and say, 'Here I am.' Or you can walk into the room and say, 'There you are.'"

I think Paul had the same mindset that Jesus had. Jesus walked into an environment and said, "There you are. Let me serve you." He healed the sick, he calmed the storm, he fed the multitudes, and he raised the dead. Wherever he went, he was a servant.

Paul concludes the chapter by encouraging the Philippians to conduct themselves in a way that is worthy of the gospel of Christ. By their conduct they would be a source of joy to other believers, whether Paul was able to come see them or not.

Paul moved from joy to joy—joy at the thought of living, joy at the thought of dying, joy at the thought of continuing to serve other people. Above all, he knew that this earth was not his final destination—heaven was his true home.

JOY IN UNITY

IF YOU HAVE ANY ENCOURAGEMENT FROM BEING UNITED WITH CHRIST, IF ANY COMFORT FROM HIS LOVE, IF ANY FELLOWSHIP WITH THE SPIRIT, IF ANY TENDERNESS AND COMPASSION, THEN MAKE MY JOY COMPLETE BY BEING LIKE-MINDED, HAVING THE SAME LOVE, BEING ONE IN SPIRIT AND PURPOSE.

—PHILIPPIANS 2:1–2

We often use phrases such as, "You know what I'm saying?" "You got my drift?" "Are we on the same page?" "Do you know where I'm coming from?" What we really want to know is, "Are we together, are we unified?"

Unity does not come from without, but from within. Unity comes from an allegiance to the same purpose, the same goals—and an allegiance to Christ. Unity is a state of harmony.

We know that the Philippian church had some problems with unity. A couple of women were having some problems which Paul needed to address. Paul was not angry. These people were very dear to him, and he loved them because of the bond he had shared with them. Many of these people were led to Christ through Paul. Yet he had intensity in his tone, because he did not want this little problem to grow. He reminded them—and us—that we truly need to understand Christ's humility and what he has done for us.

Paul gave us a list of characteristics we should have in common. He was not talking about uniformity, where we all act the same, dress the same, and behave the same. That would bring about excess and legalism. A list of rules and regulations would not create unity. Remembering how Jesus thought, acted, and taught would cause them to be unified. Paul was referring to unity that comes from the heart, from understanding a Christ-filled life.

United with Christ

Human beings tend to rally around something they have in common. People rally around a candidate who shares their values. People rally around issues like abortion, joining with those who share common beliefs. For me, I rally around guys who have the same kind of motorcycle.

We all have various things that create a bond between us, but there is something that goes beyond just our thoughts and ideology. We have a bond with people because we are all human beings on this earth. When we hear about an earthquake in Iran killing thirty thousand people, we feel compassion for them, because we have a common bond as humans.

One time I was walking through the airport in Hong Kong, and I saw an elderly Buddhist priest. He was struggling with his bags, trying to get up the stairs. I walked over, picked up a couple bags, and we walked together up the stairs. He couldn't speak my language and I couldn't speak his, but he smiled and I smiled back. Why did I help him out? Because he's a human being.

But Paul says that it goes beyond the fact that we are human beings—our unity comes from the fact that we have the same Savior. The first thing that should unify us is Christ. Jesus is our bond. It's a great thrill in life to meet people of other walks of life and people of other denominations who have Jesus as the center of their life.

Several pastors in my area have started to meet at each other's churches in order to pray for the ministry of each church. It is a privilege to participate in this. There is such joy from being with others of like mind, even though we are from different denominations. We don't agree on every doctrine, but Jesus binds us together.

In 1 Corinthians 12, Paul explains that we are all members of one body. In Philippians 2, he is reminding the Philippian church of a similar thing: that their focus should be on the one thing they *all* have in common—Christ.

Comfort in Christ

Next, Paul says that we are united by the comfort of Christ's love. The New International Version translation uses the word "if." In the original Greek, this word actually means "since" or "if, and it is assumed to be true." So Paul is really saying, in effect, "*Since* you have received this comfort."

Have you experienced the comfort of Jesus? Not the kind that comes through the ministry of others, or through reading the Bible, but the quietness of your own heart and soul, the comfort of Jesus at a point in life when things are very difficult?

Do you remember the story of Hannah in 1 Samuel? She wanted a child very much, but she was barren. Her husband's other wife harassed Hannah constantly and mocked her because of her barrenness. The Bible says that this went on year after year. The New International Version says that Hannah was in "bitterness of soul." She cried out to the Lord in this bitterness of soul because she wanted a child.

Have you had a time like that in your life, that "bitterness of soul," when everything looks dark all around you? That time when, before your head even hits the pillow, tears begin to fall and you weep because something inside of you is so painful, so distressing, and so dark that you can't even verbalize it.

Maybe somebody has rejected you, maybe you found out that your spouse wants to get a divorce, maybe there's a schism between you and your family that just haunts you. Maybe you're feeling guilty because you've done something that no one knows about except you. Maybe, like Hannah, you are mourning over something you want but do not have.

Maybe it's because of a loss. You've lost a family member, a spouse, or a close friend, and you are grieving. Maybe it's because of deep regret. You would like to turn back the clock and do it all over, but the only thing that you can do is cry before the Lord. That is when the comfort of Christ comes to us. I cannot give you that comfort. Your friends cannot give you that comfort. Only the comfort of Christ can deal with the darkness of the soul.

I have found that when Christ comes to me in my darkest hours—and I've certainly had mine—he doesn't come in long paragraphs and flowery sentences. You'll find the voice of Christ comes to you in very short and quiet phrases. "I am with you now." "I will never leave you or forsake you."

Paul phrases it beautifully in 2 Corinthians 1:3–4: "Praise be to the God and Father of our Lord Jesus Christ, the Father of compassion and the God of all comfort, who comforts us in all our troubles, so that we can comfort those in any trouble with the comfort we ourselves have received from God." Do you allow God to comfort you in all your troubles?

I watched a program on television in which a person said that if you are experiencing depression for longer than three or four days you need to go to a doctor and get some medicine. I don't doubt that there are those who have chemical imbalances and need medicine. I am not against medication or seeking medical help. But many times we are way too fast to get medication that will alter our moods and make us a little bit happier, masking the real issue God wants to address. If we only look to other things to comfort us and not to God, when will we have the opportunity to experience the comfort of Christ?

As my wife, Deb, and I watched this program, she said to me, "I've thought of doing that sometimes." She certainly had reason to be depressed. She had an unplanned child at forty. Then, a few months later, we packed up and moved, far away from all her old friends, to a new place. I can remember a period of time in her life for about a year when life was really dark. But she explained to me, "That was the time I could have gone to the doctor and gotten some drugs, but God had to work in me and deal with things in my life."

How easy it is to raise our hands to the Lord and sing praise songs when everything is wonderful. Then as soon as our world takes a little bit of a turn and we're not as happy anymore, we want to alter our mood. Not by the Holy Spirit, not by the comfort of Christ, but we'd rather do what millions of other people are doing: pop a pill and think everything will be okay.

The only problem is, if you don't work through it with Jesus, when you're done with the pills, the problem is still there. He is still trying to work. He is still trying to deal with you, and often we prolong the situation by looking for other solutions.

Fellowship of the Spirit

In addition to experiencing the unity and comfort of Christ, Paul talks about something that takes a bit of time to understand: the fellowship of the Spirit—letting ourselves be led by the Spirit of God. Like many things in the Christian life, being led by the Spirit is really a life of experimentation.

One way we experiment is with our spiritual gifts. For example, I started preaching when I was nineteen and fell right on my face. However, I kept at it, taking more speech classes, and going to seminary, and hopefully one of these days I'll be good at it. We have to go through situations—experiments, if you will—where we increasingly learn to allow the Spirit to lead. As we serve in various contexts we will begin to recognize the spiritual gifts God has given us. Not only will others affirm these gifts in us, but we also will sense a joy and passion for exercising our gifts.

We also experience the Spirit's fellowship in another way. Where does our comfort come from? All the things that we struggle over and wrestle with in our own soul—the Lord knows those. Jesus says, "I'm sending you the Comforter." He promised he would send us a Comforter. The Comforter is not a pill. The

Comforter is the Holy Spirit of God. I am not telling everybody to throw away all their medication, I'm suggesting that we go after it too quickly.

It's the same thing with pain. Our Western mentality says, "My back is killing me. Do you have some Vicodine?" Instead of "Lord, my back is killing me. Will you take care of it for me?" If you walk with the Lord and you're serious about your relationship with him, you will be amazed at some of the things he will do in you physically. I'm always amazed at what happens.

Tenderness and Compassion

A poll about President George Bush revealed that people felt better about his foreign policy at the time than they did about his domestic policy. I thought to myself, *Lord, that's kind of the way we are in church as well.* All churches have their domestic and foreign policy. We may be really good at missions, but how is our domestic policy right here where we are? How are we at unity? How are we at remembering that our bond is Jesus?

When you're in pain—emotional or physical—you want somebody who's tender and compassionate. When you were a little child and you fell down and got bloody, you didn't want your parents to stand there and say, "Oh, suck it up." You wanted them to get down and say, "Oh, you poor dear. Let me take care of this."

I've had back pain off and on since I was twenty-two. So when someone tells me that pain is going down his leg and he has spasms and can't walk, I understand. I feel for him, and I have compassion for him. Paul is saying that the tenderness and compassion of Christ draws us together.

May our Christian experience be so real and dynamic that we experience Christ's comfort, his compassion, and his tenderness through the ministry of the Holy Spirit in our lives.

CHAPTER 8

JOY IN HUMILITY

DO NOTHING OUT OF SELFISH AMBITION OR VAIN CONCEIT,
BUT IN HUMILITY CONSIDER OTHERS BETTER THAN YOURSELVES.
EACH OF YOU SHOULD LOOK NOT ONLY TO YOUR
OWN INTERESTS, BUT ALSO TO THE
INTERESTS OF OTHERS.

—PHILIPPIANS 2:3–4

Americans are often criticized for being self-absorbed and conceited. Of course, no one ever says to their friends, "I am a self-centered, self-absorbed, selfish pig." We like to see ourselves in the best light possible. We all love to think of ourselves as humble servants of the Lord. People don't want to see themselves in the light of their own arrogance or pride.

In this passage, Paul deals with a touchy subject—humility. *The Message* says, "Don't push your way to the front; don't sweet-talk your way to the top. Put yourself aside, and help others get ahead. Don't be obsessed with getting your own advantage. Forget yourselves long enough to lend a helping hand."

The Romans hated the word *humility*. It was a word that showed weakness and meant submission, and the Romans were not going to be in submission to anyone else. However, Paul lifts up the word *humility*. Christians should be very familiar with this word.

Learning Humility

Several years ago I had the opportunity to speak at Creation Festival. I had longed for the day that I would get an invitation to Creation. Creation is a Christian version of Woodstock. It is gigantic. I'll never forget the day in San Diego when I got a call and the guy on the other end of the phone said, "Dan, you are going to Creation—both Creations, East and West Coast—and you're not just going to do a seminar. You are main stage."

I can remember floating off the ground that day. I was so excited about going there. It is the communicator's Mecca—seventy to ninety thousand people attend these events. The stage at Creation is massive.

When I arrived the first morning, people were gathering to worship. I was met by Harry Thomas, the Pentecostal Assembly of God pastor who started Creation. In fact, the morning I was speaking marked the twentieth anniversary of Creation festivals, and I could hardly wait.

When I got up on stage, Harry greeted me with a big hug and prayed for me. He introduced me to the huge crowd. I preached my message, doing the best I could in the power of the Lord, and I gave an invitation. Scores of people piled into the prayer tent. It was one of the most moving experiences I've ever had as an evangelist. When it was all over, Harry was there patting me on the back. "Dan, God used you this morning."

After I got back home, I was told they had sold numerous tapes and they were sending me a check for them. They said, "We're going to be inviting you back again." I thought, *This is really cool. They're going to invite me back. Lord, I'm just your humble servant. Lord, you know how few people get invited to speak at Creation. Yeah, Lord, I'm just your humble servant. I must have done pretty good because they're going to invite me back next year. Just your humble servant.*

I know what time of year they book festivals. So the next year came along, and I waited for my phone call. *I'm going back to Creation*, I thought. No phone call. But I did find out that a friend of mine got a phone call. I wasn't going back to Creation.

Robert Schuller has said, "The easiest job in the world for God is to humble a human being."[1] Isn't it the truth? I was thinking, *I'm just your humble servant, Lord*—until I didn't get invited back.

Underneath that layer of false humility was an incredible amount of pride. My heart was really saying, *Lord, I have arrived. I have made Creation main stage. Let me at 'em.*

I got an e-mail from Harry Thomas. "Dan, can you put Creation on your calendar for 2005?" Instead of jumping up and down this time and floating down the stairs, I laughed. The last time I was at Creation was in 1999. I just laughed and thought, *Lord, this is just like you. You're just going to take your time and humble me to show me where my motives really are.* God has no trouble whatsoever exposing our hearts. God took five years to make a point in my life.

James reminds us, "God opposes the proud but gives grace to the humble" (James 4:6). Jesus said, "For everyone who exalts himself will be humbled, and he who humbles himself will be exalted" (Luke 14:11). Sometimes, if we don't humble ourselves, God just has to teach us the hard way.

Understanding Who We Are

So what is humility? Where does it come from? One aspect of humility is the proper estimation of one's self.

Some people are filled with pride and arrogance and talk about themselves all the time. They never see their own wrong, and they will never admit to it. If their actions were wrong, they blame it on someone else. You and I have met those kinds of people. You and I have been one of them.

Then there is the opposite extreme, in which an individual despises himself. He literally abhors himself. That, too, is a sin of a different kind. These people cannot get their failures out of their minds—they dwell on all their shortcomings, all the things that they've done wrong. They can't move forward; they can't have joy; they can't minister to other people because they are so self-absorbed in their failures.

Whether a person is extremely proud or whether a person despises himself or herself, they are not practicing humility. Real humility is displayed by the person who is not consumed with himself or herself, but is consumed with who God is and what he has asked us to do for other people.

John Wesley wrote, "Joy that accompanies the witness of God's Spirit is a humble joy."[2] True humility brings joy. Why? Because the humble person is concerned about the Lord's work and is not consumed by how he is going to appear to other people.

Real humility not only allows us to see our sin but also leads us to repentance. It allows us to be honest with ourselves and honest with God. True humility brings change. That's the ministry of the Holy Spirit, who blows away our self-deception.

I have been married since 1978. In those years, there have been plenty of times when my wife has pointed out to me something in my life that I need to work on. Sometimes I get defensive and say, "Yeah, but …" Other times I humble myself and accept her loving correction. When I take the second route, I end up feeling so much better afterward.

Humility brings freedom. As long as we walk around like we've got it all together, like we have no weaknesses, we're just deceiving ourselves. When we submit to the correction of those who love us, not only do we show humility, but we also end up a better person.

Understanding Who Others Are

Humility also comes from a realistic appraisal of others. Paul says, "Do nothing out of selfish ambition or vain conceit." In his letter to the Romans he writes, "Be devoted to one another in brotherly love. Honor one another above yourselves" (Rom. 12:10).

This doesn't mean that we should think others are better than we are and lower our value of ourselves. It just means that we should look out for the interests of other people.

Paul gives us these specifics in Romans 12:16–18. "Live in harmony with one another. Do not be proud, but be willing to associate with people of low position. Do not be conceited. Do not repay anyone evil for evil. Be careful to do what is right in the eyes of everybody. If it is possible, as far as it depends on you, live at peace with everyone."

Does Paul mean that we should look out for the interests of *all* the other people around us? Actually, if you look at the context of this passage, Paul is not referring to someone who is not walking with the Lord. The context is about two women who are not getting along that well, but really had a deep respect for the Lord and the church.

Paul says to look out for the interest of others who are on the same path, who want to serve the Lord, and who want to see the church grow. The truly humble person serves others out of a desire to do God's will. He or she should not be concerned about rewards or the praise of others. This is not submission out of guilt and fear. This is submission out of love and appreciation.

Humility does not seek equality of behavior. Humility says, "It doesn't matter what you do back to me. I'm going to treat you this way because the Lord has asked me to treat you this way." It goes back to the words of Jesus. "Do to others what you would have them do to you." That's what Paul was talking about. Unity begins with humility, and that humility comes when we have a right estimation of who we are and who others are.

Jim Bakker was an evangelist who lost everything when he was caught in adultery and found guilty of embezzlement. Jim tells his story in the book *I Was Wrong*.

Not long after my release from prison, I joined Franklin Graham and his family at his parents' old log mountain home for dinner. Ruth Graham, Billy Graham's wife, had prepared a full course dinner. We talked and laughed and enjoyed a casual meal together like family.

During our conversation, Ruth asked me a question that required an address. I reached into my back pocket and pulled out an envelope. My wallet had been taken when I went to prison and I had not owned a wallet for over four and a half years. As I fumbled through the envelope, Ruth asked tenderly, "Don't you have a wallet, Jim?"

"This is my wallet," I replied.

Ruth left the room, returning with one of Billy's wallets. "Here. Here is a brand-new wallet Billy has never used. I want you to have it," she said.

I still carry that wallet to this day and over the years I have met thousands of wonderful Christian men and women but never anyone more humble, gracious, and in a word, "real" than Ruth Graham and her family.[3]

Thomas Merton, a Trappist monk, once said, "Pride makes us artificial and humility makes us real."[4] The question is Are we artificial or real? Are we honest with ourselves about who we are, and are we honest with God?

CHAPTER 9

DO YOU WANT TO BE LIKE JESUS?

YOUR ATTITUDE SHOULD BE THE SAME AS THAT OF CHRIST JESUS: WHO, BEING IN VERY NATURE GOD, DID NOT CONSIDER EQUALITY WITH GOD SOMETHING TO BE GRASPED, BUT MADE HIMSELF NOTHING, TAKING THE VERY NATURE OF A SERVANT, BEING MADE IN HUMAN LIKENESS. AND BEING FOUND IN APPEARANCE AS A MAN, HE HUMBLED HIMSELF AND BECAME OBEDIENT TO DEATH— EVEN DEATH ON A CROSS!

—PHILIPPIANS 2:5–8

In Christian circles, we often talk about becoming more like Jesus. We ask ourselves What would Jesus do? and we sing songs about being conformed to the image of Christ. But the question that always comes to my mind is Do I really want to be like Jesus? And if I really want to be like Jesus, what is that going to look like, and how is it going to impact my life?

In this second chapter of Philippians, we begin to see that joy comes from humility. Paul uses Jesus as the greatest example of humility.

Most Bible scholars agree that Philippians 2:5–8 was an early Christian church hymn. The debate is whether Paul wrote this hymn or whether it was written by someone else and Paul just incorporated it into this passage.

I love this passage of Scripture because it really tells us what the early church thought of Jesus. It gives us a great glimpse into the church and what they were teaching and singing during those early years after Jesus' resurrection. Whether Paul wrote the hymn or someone else did, the words certainly gave the message that he wanted to convey to the Philippians.

We say we want to be like Jesus, but the question we each must ask is Do we really? Because if we really do, three attitudes that we see in these verses should be carried out in our Christian lives: submission, service, and sacrifice.

Submission

Verses 5 and 6 tell us that our attitude should be one of submission. Submitting to anything or anyone goes against our nature. It reveals the pride in our soul. We don't like to submit.

Here we see Jesus submitting to God. Jesus Christ didn't need anyone. He was the designer and the sustainer of all living things. Yet, at this point in time he submits, because he didn't see his equality with God as something that he needed to selfishly hold on to.

Jesus willingly came to earth because he desired to redeem the human race. Jesus came because he was interested in others—because he was interested in you.

It's been said that a lot of people can handle responsibility, but if you really want to see a person's true character, give them a privilege. Privilege is a difficult thing to deal with. In 2002, a huge scandal occurred with a company named Enron that displayed that. In short, the greed of a few high up in the company devastated the lives of many workers. A man with incredible wealth is now in big trouble because he could not handle the privilege.

Satan also had a great privilege as the highest angel, but he abused it. He wanted recognition and worship. Jesus was just the opposite. Instead of using his privilege as God's Son to lord it over people, he had an attitude of submission.

If we truly want to be like Jesus, we must address these questions: Where do we submit? Does our submission show up in our relationships, at church, with people at work, and within our family?

Service

The God who made all and knows all became one of his own creations. To me that's an amazing thing. Where is the spectacle of the pageantry, the glory, and the power? Jesus doesn't come that way. He comes as a servant. The word here in Philippians 2:7 actually means "slave." He comes not just as a "servant of the Lord," but as a slave, ready to serve.

Jesus was born in a village that had no notoriety whatsoever. His first visitors were shepherds who were looked down upon and had no standing within the community. His birth was suspicious, born of a virgin. His first house was a stable and his first bed a manger.

Where was the spectacular ceremony? Where were the well-dressed men? Where were the press conferences? Where were the power lunches? No, Jesus came to serve. Mark 10:45 says, "For even the Son of Man did not come to be served, but to serve, and to give his life as a ransom for many."

Jesus and his disciples served fishermen, prostitutes, swindlers, and social outcasts. They spent time with the sick and the weak. Jesus washed his disciples' feet like a common house slave. This is the same attitude that we are supposed to have as men and women who want to be like Christ.

Most of us love to work and serve in the realm of our passions and gifting. If someone calls me and asks me to speak at a conference, I say, "Yeah, I can probably do that." That's not a great burden for me to do. It's something I enjoy doing.

However, if somebody calls me with a crisis and they want some counseling, I get a little nervous, because that's not really my greatest gift or passion. However, I think God sometimes calls us to do something that is a little outside our comfort zone. That's when we truly have to submit and we have to serve.

We can serve three ways. First of all, we can serve by doing what we like, where we like it. Let's say you are a teacher, and you really like to teach adults. Somebody calls you and asks, "Would you teach the adult Sunday school class?" Of course, you're happy to do it.

The second way we can serve is by doing what we like, but not where we like it. Someone comes and asks you to teach the children's class. You think, *Well, I like teaching, but I don't really like children very much.* Yet it is still an opportunity to serve.

The third way to serve is doing what we don't like, in a place that we don't like. Now that's a little more difficult. Again, assume your spiritual gift is teaching and someone asks you, "Will you host these people in your home?" Now that's the gift of hospitality. Unfortunately, hospitality is not your strong point, and people will soon find that out when they get to your home.

When it comes to serving, sometimes we get to do exactly what we want to do, exactly where we want to do it, and then there are times when we don't get to do what we like best.

Although he came to serve, do you think Jesus enjoyed the thought of dying and going through all that pain? You might be serving in a place where you don't feel gifted, but God is still using you and still blessing you because you've said, "I will submit and serve."

"Each of you should look not only to your own interests, but also to the interests of others," Paul says in verse 4.

My wife likes crafts. We've been married twenty-five years and I still hate crafts. There is no love for crafts in my soul, and I don't pretend that there is. But Deb also likes antiques. I don't care that much for antiques, and I always want to stop at the Harley store while she wants to stop at an antique store. In twenty-five years, I think we've gone to ten thousand antique stores. As we've grown together, this is one area where I have started to become interested simply because it's an interest of hers.

Being interested in the other person is so important in a marriage. It's not enough to simply have two Christians, even though sometimes I think that is what our mentality is. But a person can be a Christian and not be Christlike at all. You have to look at his or her life, and ask some tough questions. Does this guy exemplify Christ? Is this girl submissive to authority and to the Lord? Does she like to serve? Will he look out for the interests of others?

Anybody can go to church on Sunday morning. Get out of bed, put your clothes on, drive to church, and sit there. That's easy. In everyday life, you see the true side of a person. We each have to ask ourselves: Am I really a follower of Jesus? Do I have the same attitude of submission and service that he had?

Sacrifice

The third characteristic of Jesus that we can emulate is his attitude of sacrifice. In verse 8, Paul explains how Jesus humbled himself and became obedient to death. He sacrificed for us, and not only did he willingly die, but he submitted to a disgraceful death. Death by crucifixion was a cruel way to die. The Jews looked at death on a cross as a curse from God.

We say, "I want to be like Jesus," yet the word *sacrifice* is something we shy away from. Sacrifice means that there is going to be a price to pay and pain will be involved. If I sacrifice, it means that I'm going to be uncomfortable, that I'm going to have to wait until another day for what I want or maybe never get it at all. It means that I'm not going to be able to be in control, but it does mean that I truly want to follow Jesus.

In Luke 9:23, Jesus tells us, "If anyone would come after me, he must deny himself and take up his cross daily and follow me."

I have a friend who serves as an evangelist in India. He goes into the rural villages and preaches Christ. He has been beaten on more than one occasion, and often receives death threats from angry mobs. He is away from his family for months on end. I think, *Wow, that's sacrifice.* But he does it gladly and willingly.

You never see Jesus grumbling about the sacrifice. "Being found in appearance as a man, he humbled himself and became obedient to death—even death on a cross." Do you want to be like Jesus? Do you submit? Do you serve even when it's not fun to serve? Have you really sacrificed?

On a trip to Romania a few years ago, I landed in the airport to discover that it was twenty degrees below zero. I was dressed like a typical Californian, in shorts and a T-shirt. A gentleman who looked about sixty years old met me at the airport. He came bundled in warm winter clothes, and when he saw how I was dressed, he insisted that I take his jacket and hat and put them on before we went outside.

As we walked together, I asked him about his life, and I found out he was actually only forty years old, but time in prison had aged him quickly. He had been beaten and starved because of the gospel, but he had never stopped sharing Christ. I was amazed and humbled. I had come to this country to teach the pastors, but they taught me far more about what it really means to live a life of sacrifice.

In reality, my sacrifice is nothing compared to what Jesus sacrificed. David Livingstone, a missionary to Africa, is reported to have made the following comment after someone praised him for his sacrifice of leaving his family and risking death for Christ. He said, "Can that be called sacrifice which is simply paid back as a small part of a great debt owed to our God, which we can never repay? It is emphatically no sacrifice; say rather it is a privilege. Anxiety, sickness, suffering, danger ... all these are nothing when compared with the glory which shall hereafter be revealed in, and for, us. I never made a sacrifice. Of this we ought not to talk, when we remember the great sacrifice which HE made who left his Father's throne on high to give himself for us."

As people look at us, do they see any resemblance to Jesus at all? They should see those attitudes of submission, service, and sacrifice in our lives. Do we want to be like Jesus? It's easy to say and it's simple to sing, but to really mean it and to really live it takes the ministry of the Holy Spirit in our lives.

CHAPTER 10

WE BOW DOWN

THEREFORE GOD EXALTED HIM TO THE HIGHEST PLACE AND GAVE HIM THE NAME THAT IS ABOVE EVERY NAME, THAT AT THE NAME OF JESUS EVERY KNEE SHOULD BOW, IN HEAVEN AND ON EARTH AND UNDER THE EARTH, AND EVERY TONGUE CONFESS THAT JESUS CHRIST IS LORD, TO THE GLORY OF GOD THE FATHER.

—PHILIPPIANS 2:9–11

The apostle John paints a beautiful picture in Revelation 7:9–10 of what heaven will be like. "After this I looked and there before me was a great multitude that no one could count, from every nation, tribe, people and language, standing before the throne and in front of the Lamb. They were wearing white robes and were holding palm branches in their hands. And they cried out in a loud voice: 'Salvation belongs to our God, who sits on the throne, and to the Lamb.'"

In his own writings, Paul makes it very clear that we will *all* bow down. The angels and the demons are going to bow down. All humans will bow down, whether they have been dead for a long time or they're alive until Jesus comes back. Every created being will bow down before the Lord Jesus Christ. What an awesome thought!

Why will we bow down? Because God will exalt Jesus to the highest place. The word *exalted* could actually be translated "super exalted." He is above all. There is nothing and no one higher than Jesus. At his name, all will bow down. Most scholars say that Paul is referring to the title "Lord" because God exalted Christ to that incredible position, "Lord of all." God exalted him because of his incredible obedience, his death, and his atoning work.

In Romans 14:11–12, Paul says, "It is written: 'As surely as I live,' says the Lord, 'every knee will bow before me; every tongue will confess to God.' So then, each of us will give an account of himself to God." However, I don't believe that we will all bow in the same way. While some of us will be bowing in adoration and love, others will bow out of compulsion.

Seeds on the Path

Some will bow down defiantly and hesitantly confess to the Lord, "Okay, you were right." There will be no submission or humility on their part. They might not even admit that they were wrong. We know people who will bow before the Lord in a defiant manner, not because they want to, but because they have to.

In Matthew 13, Jesus tells the parable of the different kinds of soil. At the end, he explains what the different kinds of soil mean. Verse 19 says, "When anyone hears the message about the kingdom and does not understand it, the evil one comes and snatches away what was sown in his heart. This is the seed sown along the path." Some might hear the truth but never grasp it. They never submit to that truth.

I think of people like Stalin, Hitler, and Saddam Hussein. How will it be for them when they realize that they are nothing in this universe and that they are now being called upon to bow down before the true Lord?

How will it be for the super-rich of the world, those who only care about money or material possessions? Some people have more money than I could imagine or could even wish for in this life. Their money has been their security and mark on this world. How will it be for those kinds of people when they see the Lord and the Lord requires them to bow down?

How will it be for the entertainers and big-time athletes who are so used to having people idolize and practically worship them? How will it be for them when they stand before the Lord and all their adoring fans don't even notice them because the radiance of the Lord is so brilliant?

How will it be for those who have lived their lives with no responsibility and no care about what God thinks? Will they bow before the Lord in adoration and appreciation? Or will it be in defiance? Those who have said, "There is no morality; there is no right or wrong," will also have to bow down.

People who hate God and mock him will be bowing defiantly before the throne. Those are the people so evil, so depraved, that at the end of their lives they absolutely cannot repent. The Bible says that God literally hardens their heart. Like the Puritan John Owen wrote, "The most tremendous judgment of God in this world is the hardening of the heart of men."[1]

Seeds on Rocky Soil

Others will bow down regretfully and confess, "I was wrong." I hate regrets. You wish you could undo something. You missed an opportunity or you spoke words falsely and you'd like to pull those words back in but you can't. We have regrets about how we've lived, what we've said, how we've behaved, or how we've reared our children. Those regrets can haunt us.

I cannot imagine the regret of the person who came to church, heard of Jesus, who knew of God's goodness and kindness and yet would not turn to the Lord. They will be thinking, *If only I had listened, if only I had said yes to the Lord.*

I believe there will be people, including churchgoers, who will stand before the Lord and be in this situation. These are the people who show up on Sunday mornings, but have no intention of getting to know him better. They have no intention of becoming a different person or changing in any manner.

Look again at Matthew 13. In verses 20–21, Jesus describes this kind of person. "The one who received the seed that fell on rocky places is the man who hears the word and at once receives it with joy. But since he has no root, he lasts only a short time. When trouble or persecution comes because of the word, he quickly falls away."

Some people come to the Lord because their emotions get all stirred up, but their will has never changed. To become a follower of Jesus, three things have to be working together: my emotions, my mind, and my will that says, "Lord, I want to follow you."

As an evangelist, I'm well aware that you can give an invitation and people will come forward, crying, hugging, and overflowing with emotion, but those same people could be long gone in three to six months. It's a frightening thought.

Several years ago, I was in Bucharest, Romania, doing an evangelistic ministry. The people there love classical music, and we were holding our meetings in the national state theater. On the last night of our ministry, a young man came forward and gave his heart to the Lord.

Years later I received an e-mail from one of the leaders in Bucharest. I found out that this same young man who came to Christ now travels all over the country and writes music for the Lord. He sings on television, in front of great leaders, and gives a testimony of what Jesus Christ has done in his life. That's the kind of story you want to hear when someone comes to the Lord.

But there will always be some who are just temporary disciples. These are nice people who get excited and come to church for a while, but it doesn't take root.

Jesus also talks about the kind of people who get upset by the worries of worldly things that snuff out their spiritual growth.

These will also be bowing down regretfully. As Charles Spurgeon preached, "Neither prayer nor praise, nor hearing of the Word will be pleasant or profitable to persons who have left their hearts behind them."[2]

Seeds in the Good Soil

Finally, there will be a few who will bow down joyfully and confess, "You are my Lord." Jesus says that these are the people who receive the word and understand it. These will produce a crop yielding a hundred or sixty or thirty times what was sown (Matt. 13:23).

Jesus makes it very clear that the true mark of Christianity, the true mark of devotion to him, is one who is producing the fruit of the Spirit. In John 6:66, we see that many of Jesus' disciples turned back and stopped following him because his teachings were too hard. The true followers of Jesus are the ones who remain until the end. These are the ones who will bow joyfully.

To these people, bowing and confessing will not seem strange at all. They are comfortable confessing: confessing their sin, confessing what they believe about God, confessing what they feel about the Lord. They are very familiar and comfortable with bowing down, because privately, in their own life, they bow before the Lord.

These Christians are familiar with Jesus. They are familiar with his words. Not only are they familiar with him, but they are also familiar with expressing worship by confessing, and familiar with bowing before the Lord.

Paul writes that *every* knee will bow. Are we going to do so defiantly, regretfully, or joyfully?

Hyde Park, in London, England, has a place called "Speaker's Corner," which became popular in the mid-1800s. Many famous people have spoken there, standing on the soapbox and shouting out over the crowd.

One man at Speaker's Corner said, "People tell me that God exists, but I can't see him. People tell me there is life after death, but I can't see it. People tell me that there is judgment to come, but I can't see it. People tell me that there is a heaven and a hell, but I can't see them." He got off the soapbox and people clapped.

Then another man walked up, and after he was assisted in climbing up to the soapbox, he said calmly, "People tell me there is green grass all around here, but I can't see it. People tell me that there is blue sky above, but I can't see it. People tell me that there are trees nearby, but I can't see them. You see, I'm blind."

As I read that story, I thought, *Lord, may you remove any spiritual blindness that we might have. May we feel great freedom to bow before you, to worship you, and to confess to you what we believe.*

How do you bow? Do you bow defiantly? "Grrrrr." Do you bow regretfully? "Oh, man …" Or do you bow joyfully? "Hallelujah. I worship you, Lord. I praise your name. I exalt you because you are Lord of heaven and earth." Are we going to be that soil that receives Jesus with gladness and bears fruit?

CHAPTER 11

ARE YOU A SHINING STAR?

*THEREFORE, MY DEAR FRIENDS, AS YOU HAVE ALWAYS OBEYED—
NOT ONLY IN MY PRESENCE, BUT NOW MUCH MORE IN MY
ABSENCE—CONTINUE TO WORK OUT YOUR SALVATION WITH FEAR
AND TREMBLING, FOR IT IS GOD WHO WORKS IN YOU TO WILL
AND TO ACT ACCORDING TO HIS GOOD PURPOSE.*

*DO EVERYTHING WITHOUT COMPLAINING OR ARGUING, SO THAT YOU
MAY BECOME BLAMELESS AND PURE, CHILDREN OF GOD WITHOUT
FAULT IN A CROOKED AND DEPRAVED GENERATION, IN WHICH YOU
SHINE LIKE STARS IN THE UNIVERSE AS YOU HOLD OUT THE WORD OF
LIFE—IN ORDER THAT I MAY BOAST ON THE DAY OF CHRIST THAT I
DID NOT RUN OR LABOR FOR NOTHING. BUT EVEN IF I AM BEING
POURED OUT LIKE A DRINK OFFERING ON THE SACRIFICE AND SERVICE
COMING FROM YOUR FAITH, I AM GLAD AND REJOICE WITH ALL OF
YOU. SO YOU TOO SHOULD BE GLAD AND REJOICE WITH ME.*

—PHILIPPIANS 2:12–18

A fire station in Livermore, California, holds the Guinness world record for the longest burning light bulb. A four-watt bulb has been burning since 1901. Each year, they have a celebration for the light bulb in order to mark another birthday. I'm sure the firemen who keep watch over this historical landmark must be getting nervous that it will burn out someday soon.[1]

Even brighter than the strongest light bulb are our stars. We have stars of all sizes in our universe. The sun is actually one of the smaller ones, even though it could hold 1.3 million earths. Despite their varying sizes, each star has a life cycle—they are birthed, they live, and then they die. Although some will burn for longer than others, eventually every star burns out. And if the Lord doesn't return before then, our sun will burn up too.

Paul builds this passage around the idea of shining stars, comparing Christians to stars in the universe. He is concerned about his brothers' and sisters' lights not shining properly. In their spiritual life cycles, they are moving towards the end, threatening to burn out.

The moment that we open our hearts to Jesus and invite him in is the moment we first begin to shine. Do you remember the point when you came to the Lord? Was it apparent that the Holy Spirit was in you and that you were not the same person? The light of Christ should be reflected in our lives from the moment we become Christians. When did you begin to shine?

Up to this point, the Philippian church had been a strong light. They had a great testimony and other people were coming to know Jesus because of them. Their eyes were focused on heaven. C. S. Lewis has said that those who did the most for this world were those who thought the most about the next.[2] If I am a shining light, how committed am I to the next world—to eternity?

A horrible tragedy recently occurred for a family in Portland, Oregon. An associate pastor of a large church was fatally shot by his own son. They got into an argument because the boy was on drugs, and the son shot his dad in the chest, killing him.

This pastor's wife has not only lost her husband, but she will also lose her son because he will be in prison for many years. I realized that in my American mindset, I value life above anything else. However, God does not see it that way. He sees our spirits as more important than our bodies. Yes, it is a horrible tragedy that this pastor died, but now he is in heaven with Jesus. The spirit is the most important because it is eternal.

A Fading Light

I believe Paul was concerned about the Philippians because their light was beginning to dim. They were having some disunity in the church, and their testimony was weakening. We all have times in our lives when our lights don't shine as brightly as other times.

What was making the Philippians' light dim? Paul says, "Therefore, my dear friends, as you have always obeyed—not only in my presence, but now much more in my absence— continue to work out your salvation with fear and trembling" (v. 12). When Paul was with them, they had obeyed well. But now that he is gone, he is concerned that their obedience might be slipping.

We spend years training our kids, disciplining them, and teaching them to be obedient. At some point, we give them the test—we leave them alone for a few hours and see if they can behave by themselves as well in our absence as they have behaved in our presence. Often the first few times, they don't make it. They end up sneaking into the freezer for some ice cream or watching a TV show they shouldn't. Then you have to start the process over again.

The Philippian church was beginning to slip now that Paul had left. They were complaining and arguing, and Paul reminds them that children of God should not be known for grumbling. In his absence, they had become sidetracked. Paul already knew that he would soon be dealing with two women who were causing some division in the church. The light was beginning to dim.

In Numbers 14, we see how much God hates grumbling and complaining. When the Israelites began to grumble against Moses, God was so irritated that he wanted to destroy them and start over with Moses.

Complaining is as much a problem in the church as any-where else. I read about a church that was being sued by some of the members because they wanted their hymns back. At another church, the pastor is suing the elders for firing him over some of his questionable behavior.

Grumbling, fighting, and complaining distract us from the task. They sidetrack us from what we should be doing. Instead of shining forth a light into the community, we are focused on internal disputes.

Is there a time in your life when your light began to dim? My light started dimming in my thirties. Up to that point, I had been faithful about sharing Christ, and I lived to see others come to know the Lord. Ironically, when I began to work for an evangelistic association, my fire began to die because I had become a "professional" in the area of evangelism. I grew so concerned with the programs and procedures that I became sidetracked. I have had to go to the Lord on several occasions and confess that my light has dimmed.

Philip Yancey wrote a wonderful article about the life cycle of the Christian community. He said that we discipline our-selves in our money, our work ethic, and our lives in order to be successful. This brings us abundance and blessing. Yet, over time this blessing turns to a curse because the blessing becomes more important than the discipline was. Yancey says, "We continue to run in this cycle with Christianity within America of discipline, blessing, and decadence, where the Christian community just continues to live like everybody else does."[3]

What things in our culture get into our lives and cause the light to dim? That's what Paul was concerned about. He says, "Work out your salvation." That doesn't mean work for your salvation, but take a look at what is working and what is not working about your faith. Don't blame your failings on others or on the church, but recognize the areas you need to work on. Believers continually working on their salvation and developing their dependence on God will be brightly shining lights.

A New Fire

If your light was once burning brightly but now has begun to dim, what will it take to make it shine again? What do we need to do to bravely hold forth the word of life?

Wouldn't it be great if we could wake up on Monday morning and say, "Lord, who can I bring closer to you this week?" Instead of thinking about getting to work on time or what bills need to be paid, wouldn't it be great if we could focus our week on where to shine our light?

If every Christian in your city were killed except you, would you be able to march forward? Could you be a shining light to lead others to Christ and rebuild the church? That is a convicting thought for me. Knowledge without power will never transform a community. Dogma and creed without love will never transform a community. Only Christ's love shining through his people will draw others to the truth.

Martin Luther King Jr. gave a wonderful sermon in which he encouraged believers to establish a colony of heaven here on earth. In it he said, "Most Christians are thermometers that record or register the temperature of majority opinion, not thermostats that transform and regulate the temperature of society."[4] We need to be the ones who determine what our society will look like.

Jesus said that he came to seek and to save what was lost. As obedient followers, we should do the same. Our ministry is to hold forth the word of life, and shine as bright stars in a dark world.

In Matthew 5:14–16, Jesus says, "You are the light of the world. A city on a hill cannot be hidden.... Let your light shine before men, that they may see your good deeds and praise your Father in heaven." We are clearly called to be light to nonbelievers.

Let me give you a challenge. If you don't think about the lost, if you never try to share your faith with anyone, then you are not being an obedient follower of Jesus. Perhaps your light has grown dim, or maybe it has never gotten strong, but you can fan that flame right now by making a commitment to be a witness for Jesus.

When a star burns out, it doesn't come back. When a light bulb burns out, we throw it away. But praise God that he brings back burned-out Christians. Even the person with the coldest heart who has lost his or her way can come back to God, who will relight the fire in our souls.

The Philippian church began with a bright light and a strong witness in their community. However, that light was beginning to dim because of the bickering and arguing that was taking place within the church.

As the church—the body of believers—we need to watch out for this trap. In Revelation 3, Jesus rebukes the church at Laodicea for being lukewarm. Their light had grown dim because they had been choked out by the world and its pleasures. Jesus told them to repent, to go back to the way they had been when their light first started to shine.

For many years when I lived in San Diego, California, we had a Christmas Eve tradition in our community. Volunteers would bring white paper bags, sand, and tea lights to each house. On Christmas Eve we would fill the bags with sand and nestle the tea lights inside, then place fifteen to twenty of them on the sidewalk in front of each of our homes.

When it got dark we would all go out and light the candles, and the neighborhood would be transformed. The streets were lined with these beautiful luminaries, and as you walked down the road, you truly felt like you were in a winter wonderland. We enjoyed a wonderful evening, but eventually the candles would burn out, and by midnight it would once again be dark.

What is your heart like? Is it cold? Have the lights gone out? No matter what may have caused you to grow dim, you can always come to the Lord and say, "Relight the fire in my heart. Here are the things that have been blocking my way. Please give me a new passion to love you and reach the lost for you."

As we come to the Lord and open up before him and confess our shortcomings, he fills us anew with his Holy Spirit. The Spirit fans the flame and brings us back to the brightness we once had.

At some point, the light of Christ shining in someone else led you to accept him. Now will you be that light to others? It doesn't matter if we're shy or our gifts are different or if our personalities are not very bold. Let's be living luminaries who bring a warm glow to the dark paths of people's hearts!

Chapter 12

You've Got a Friend

I hope in the Lord Jesus to send Timothy to you soon, that I also may be cheered when I receive news about you. I have no one else like him, who takes a genuine interest in your welfare. For everyone looks out for his own interests, not those of Jesus Christ. But you know that Timothy has proved himself, because as a son with his father he has served with me in the work of the gospel. I hope, therefore, to send him as soon as I see how things go with me. And I am confident in the Lord that I myself will come soon.

—*Philippians 2:19–24*

C. S. Lewis said, "Friendship is born at the moment when one person says to another, 'What? You too. I thought I was the only one.'"[1] That's what a soul mate is—someone to whom you can say, "This is where I am. This is how I feel. These are the doubts that I have." And the person says, "That's okay. I've been there myself." Timothy was just that kind of friend to Paul.

It's interesting to note that Paul and Timothy really were quite different. Often our closest friends have a different temperament, different interests, and different gifts than we do. Sometimes you might look at some of your friends and be unable to figure out why they're your friends.

Paul was the boss; Timothy was the worker. Paul was older; Timothy was younger. Paul was aggressive; Timothy was timid. Paul was a leader; Timothy was a shepherd. Paul was a Type-A personality and Timothy was anything but that. Yet they were very close, and Paul says about Timothy, "I have no one else like him."

Paul and Timothy had built this close friendship through their many years together sharing the gospel. Timothy became Paul's right-hand man. Paul later wrote two important letters to Timothy, calling him "my dear son" and "my true son in the faith." He loved Timothy as he would his own child, and he poured much time and energy into training him and preparing him for an effective ministry.

Paul wanted the Philippians to know how he was doing and he wanted to know how they were doing, so he sent a couple of his buddies to check on them. These weren't acquaintances or just any friends, but they were Paul's soul mates. In our lifetime, we only get to have a few soul mates, people that we can truly be ourselves with and speak what is on our mind or in our hearts. Paul was especially blessed to have Timothy as a friend.

Friend of the Philippians

Paul was sending a familiar person to the church at Philippi. Timothy had worked there before, and he knew the story and situation of the Philippians. Having just dealt with the issues of grumbling and complaining in the previous verses, I think Paul moved on to talking about Timothy because Timothy was not a grumbler or complainer. Timothy had true character. He was living out the life of Jesus.

Sometimes, like Timothy, we are sent by a friend or mentor to minister in their place. I was in Wales in 1989, helping out with the evangelistic ministry of Luis Palau. We had been there for several weeks when one night Luis came to me. "Dan, I think you should preach Friday night," he said. "I need a break, and the experience would be good for you." I agreed to preach that night, so Luis picked up the phone and called the chairman. "I'm not feeling well tonight, so my Timothy, Dan Owens, is going to step in and take my place."

As I got up on stage that night, I was excited, but also nervous because I had doubts about how the audience would respond since I was not the advertised speaker. Sure enough, right after they introduced me and explained that Luis was taking the night off, several people got up and walked out. I knew that might happen, but I continued on.

One thing working in my favor was my last name. Owens is a very Welch name. In fact, Daniel Richard Owens is about as Welch as you can get. I tried to play that up a bit, then I went on to give the message and an invitation. It was a great time.

That day in 1989 became one of the most cherished times of my ministry because of a sixty-one-year-old man who heard the gospel and invited me to come to his house and talk with him about the Lord. He accepted Christ that day, and it was a great thrill for me to be involved.

As Timothy went in Paul's place, he knew there might be some people who would be disappointed. But they knew of Timothy's proven character. It wasn't just about personality. In America we get really attached to that. If we like a person's personality, we'll hang around him or her; otherwise, we move on to the next person.

During my first couple weeks as the new pastor at a church, I had a couple come up and say to me, "We liked the pastor before you better, so we're leaving." But for the church at Philippi, it wasn't that way. They saw Timothy as a man of character, a man who cared for them and loved them, and they were going to accept him gladly.

Friend of Christ

Paul had many friends and fellow workers. But not all of them were as committed to Christ's interests as Timothy. Paul alludes to such individuals when he writes, "For everyone looks out for his own interests, not those of Jesus Christ" (v. 21). One man, Demas, is mentioned in Colossians 4:14 and again in Philemon 1:24. He is described as a good man, serving alongside Paul. He experienced all the miracles and saw what God was doing. But then something happened. Paul says that Demas loved this present world too much, and it caused him to desert the ministry of the gospel (2 Tim. 4:10).

Demas was a friend of Paul, and a friend of Christ, but something happened and he ended up walking away from it all. That still happens to Christians today.

I received an e-mail from a friend who is a pastor and has been mentoring a young man in his faith. He had just found out that this young disciple turned his back on God, left his wife and his friends, and went back to his old life. What a disappointment!

Demas was sidetracked. Was he sidetracked by worldly pleasures and sin? I used to think so, but as I looked at it a little more closely, I saw something else.

The text says that Demas "loved this world." Demas loved this present world more than he loved Jesus. When did Demas forsake Paul? When Paul was put in prison, Demas must have thought, *This is not what I signed up for. I didn't sign up to be a martyr—I'm going back home where it is safe and secure.*

How many people have come to Jesus thinking that everything is going to be wonderful? How can everything be wonderful when the moment you become a Christian you become the sworn enemy of hell? How in the world can that be wonderful?

Does the Lord bless us? Absolutely. Does he love us? Of course. But there are also difficulties in this world. There are difficulties in this Christian life. Jesus told us to look at the cost of becoming a Christian and if the price tag is too high, forget it, because this is going to cost you.

Demas was a friend of Jesus, but the price was too high, so Demas went back home. I am convicted by that. Would we give it all up for this friendship that we have with Jesus? Am I really his friend? Would I really say, "Lord, where do you want to send me?"

In stark contrast to Demas, Timothy was a genuine friend of Christ. He was willing to stick it out through the tough times. In fact, Paul mentions Timothy in most of his epistles, and Timothy stays faithful to the very end. Paul wanted the Philippians to know that Timothy was a true servant as well as a friend of Jesus.

Friend of Paul

Timothy was one of Paul's soul mates. He was as close as his own flesh and blood. Paul said, "As a son with his father he has served with me in the work of the gospel." Timothy had proven himself faithful, and Paul knew that he could send Timothy in his place because he was trustworthy.

In the song "You've Got a Friend" by Carol King, a line says, "Ain't it good to know that you've got a friend, when people can be so cold, they'll hurt you and desert you." Paul could have easily said those words. "They deserted me. They forsook me." But Timothy stayed by him.

I can imagine that whenever Paul and Timothy saw each other their faces lit up. I'm still good friends with one of my roommates from college, Terry. A few years ago, he gave me a BMW, so I think of him every day when I get in my car. When I see Terry I just want to laugh, because I remember all the times we had and memories we shared. We can always pick up right where we left off. Friends stay with you.

A short time ago, one of my close friends went through a difficult time in his life. Many who called themselves Christians turned their backs on him. Yet, I stayed with him because he was my friend, and I knew he would have done the same for me. Eventually, he got through his situation and is serving the Lord again. He told me, "Everybody else walked out, but you walked in." We will be soul mates forever because of that time.

What kind of a friend are you? When people you call friends go through difficult times, do you walk out or walk in? Paul could be honest with Timothy. He could confess, "I'm hurting, lonely, and discouraged. I'm afraid to go up to Jerusalem," and Timothy wouldn't abandon him, because the friendship was that important.

Paul and Timothy also had a spiritual dimension to their friendship. That is such an important and overlooked aspect of a relationship. Even at church, we will talk among other believers about the weather, our kids, or our Sunday afternoon plans, but we rarely ask the tough questions: "How are you doing spiritually?" "What has God been teaching you this week?" or "How can I pray for you?"

With our non-Christian friends, we can only go as deep as our common interests and shared experiences. However, with a fellow Christian, we have the great privilege of being able to share on a personal, spiritual level.

This world is lonely and difficult when we have no friends around us. I pray that you are a friend to someone who will become your soul mate and stay with you during the difficult times.

Albert Schweitzer, the great missionary doctor, said, "Sometimes our light goes out but is blown into flame by another human being. Each of us owes deepest thanks to those who have rekindled this light."[2] When our flame goes out, when we get discouraged, are there people around us to help light the fire again? Are we ready to fan the flame of hope for others?

Always remember that you've got a friend in Jesus. When others walk out, he doesn't need to walk in, because he's been there all along. He's been there with you all along, including when you go through difficult times. He's there with you right now, if you only acknowledge him. You've got a friend—and he's the greatest friend in the universe!

CHAPTER 13

WHEN TIMES ARE NOT JOYFUL

BUT I THINK IT IS NECESSARY TO SEND BACK TO YOU EPAPHRODITUS, MY BROTHER, FELLOW WORKER AND FELLOW SOLDIER, WHO IS ALSO YOUR MESSENGER, WHOM YOU SENT TO TAKE CARE OF MY NEEDS. FOR HE LONGS FOR ALL OF YOU AND IS DISTRESSED BECAUSE YOU HEARD HE WAS ILL. INDEED HE WAS ILL, AND ALMOST DIED. BUT GOD HAD MERCY ON HIM, AND NOT ON HIM ONLY BUT ALSO ON ME, TO SPARE ME SORROW UPON SORROW. THEREFORE I AM ALL THE MORE EAGER TO SEND HIM, SO THAT WHEN YOU SEE HIM AGAIN YOU MAY BE GLAD AND I MAY HAVE LESS ANXIETY. WELCOME HIM IN THE LORD WITH GREAT JOY, AND HONOR MEN LIKE HIM, BECAUSE HE ALMOST DIED FOR THE WORK OF CHRIST, RISKING HIS LIFE TO MAKE UP FOR THE HELP YOU COULD NOT GIVE ME.

—PHILIPPIANS 2:25–30

Too often I'm afraid we study the Bible to gather details and create a rulebook to follow. We miss the emotion of what the author wants to communicate to us. In this passage, Paul shifts from speaking with joy of his friend Timothy to displaying some anxiety over another friend, Epaphroditus. Like most of us, Epaphroditus had some major struggles in his life.

At times in our lives we wonder where the joy is. We wonder why things didn't happen the way we planned.

Sometimes we view the Bible as a victory book where everyone always has a great day, and people like the apostle Paul never wake up on the wrong side of the bed. But we know that Paul had some tough times. When he pens this letter to the Philippians, Paul is imprisoned in Rome.

Roman prisons were nothing like American prisons. The state didn't give prisoners nice orange suits and three meals a day and cable television. Prisoners had to fend for themselves, and depend on family and friends to take care of them. If they didn't have anyone bringing food and provisions, the Romans just let them starve to death.

The church at Philippi, because of their love for Paul, took up an offering for him. Then they sent Epaphroditus as their courier. I'm sure he was excited to be carrying the provisions to Paul. But then something went wrong with the plan. Epaphroditus got sick—not just a little tummy ache that can be knocked down with some Pepto-Bismol. He was sick to the point of being near death.

Life is not fair. Life does not always go as we have planned. We will often go through disappointments.

Disappointment in Situations

Many of us, when in Paul's circumstances, would certainly be disappointed with this situation. Epaphroditus is supposed to be there to take care of him, and now Paul is going to lose one of his friends, one of his soul mates.

Paul calls Epaphroditus "a brother," "a fellow worker," and a "soldier." He calls him a brother because he's a Christian. Epaphroditus is a fellow worker because he is involved in helping to minister the gospel, and he's a soldier because he suffered some sort of wound or sickness in this time of serving the Lord. Paul knew he needed to send Epaphroditus back, but surely he must have felt disappointed to see his friend leave.

You might be wondering, is God only there when we have success? Is he only with us when everything looks wonderful? Or is God sovereign even in the failures? Is God there with us when we lose a job or when we have poor health or when our children go down the wrong path? In those situations, in life's disappointments, is God present?

I love the story in Mark 4 of Jesus and his disciples in the midst of a furious storm. The waves are crashing over and the boat is starting to sink. Finally someone gets the bright idea to go ask Jesus if he can do anything. They find Jesus sleeping peacefully in the back of the boat.

The disciples are pretty upset. It looks like they're about to drown, and Jesus is sleeping right through it. Doesn't he even care? I love how the Lord lets us be honest with our emotions. Scripture shows that the disciples were obviously angry. One of the great things about being a Christian is that you can tell the Lord exactly how you feel.

I've heard people say, "When you're mad at God, just tell him." I don't know if I would go that far, because he is powerful and deserves our reverence no matter what. So I watch what I say. But we can honestly communicate our emotions during difficult times.

George Müller, a pastor and evangelist who cared for thousands of orphans in England, wrote, "Trials, obstacles, difficulties, and sometimes defeats are the very food of faith."[1] Sometimes we don't want that food, though. When things go bad, we want to fix it. We want to get away from those bad things and go back to joyful times again, forgetting that God often uses those times to fuel and feed our growing faith.

It's hard to accept difficulties, but Paul had learned to be content in whatever state he found himself. Even though his plan did not work out and Epaphroditus had to go home, God was still present, working things out.

We all know that difficulties come. If you didn't have them this week, you may have them next week. That's the way life is.

When things are going well, it's good to celebrate. The difficulties and the good times are all part of God's plan.

Disappointment with Circumstances

I feel for Epaphroditus. His church sent him to go take care of Paul, and in the process he became severely ill and almost died. He was the one who was supposed to give help and now he was the one who needed help. Talk about a difficult situation. Had we been in his situation, we might have felt we'd failed Paul, and in our minds, failed the Lord, because we were on a mission to serve the Lord and couldn't complete the task.

Maybe you have been on a short-term mission trip to another country and found yourself sick the whole time. There is nothing like being sick far away from home. I've had it happen more times than I want to remember. "Lord, I came here. I'm supposed to preach, and I can't even get out of the bathroom." It's a horrible feeling.

Sometimes when we disappoint ourselves it's just the Lord working in us. Epaphroditus couldn't help getting sick, but the Lord was working in that weakness.

I think each one of us has looked in the mirror and been disappointed with ourselves, with something we've done, or said, or harbored in our heart. Sometimes we're even disappointed in our character because of a character weakness.

Remember King David? I don't think David grew up thinking, *I'm going to walk with God and he's going to make me king. I'm going to rule and we're going to see God do great things. Then one day I'm going to commit adultery and blow it all.* He didn't plan on it happening that way. Could he have prevented it? Yes, he could have prevented it, but he messed up. I'm sure he looked at himself and was incredibly disappointed with himself and with his actions.

However, David learned from that situation, and he never did it again. Even after his many disappointments, David was still called a man after God's own heart.

When we get discouraged and disappointed in ourselves, we need to remember that God knows our failures and he is always there, willing to pick us up and put us on the right path. But we need to have a heart of repentance that comes back to him.

Disappointment with Others

In a little village in England there is a sign on a bed and breakfast cottage that reads, "Please introduce yourself to your fellow guests since we are one big happy family. Do not leave valuables in your room." Unfortunately, that's real life, isn't it? We're all one big happy family, but watch your back.

We all get disappointed by other people at times. When we do, we often don't demonstrate the attitude Paul asked the Philippian church to have—an attitude more concerned with the person than the circumstances that disappointed us.

How would many people in our churches today handle a situation like the Philippian church faced? They had taken a special offering for a missionary, and selected a man to be the messenger, but he had not been able to fully fulfill his duty. Would they have been as graciously understanding as Paul asked the Philippians to be? Would they be more concerned for the messenger than for the task that didn't get accomplished? Many would not.

We are often disappointed by other people's weaknesses. We tend to judge them based on our strengths, and we feel like we need to fix them. Often in marriage, one spouse sees a weakness in his or her spouse and wants to get rid of it. Then ten or twenty years later, they finally realize that it isn't going to change.

Peter was disappointed in Jesus. Jesus said he was going to establish a kingdom. Yet Peter is standing out in the crowd and he's looking up at the cross. *What happened, Jesus? I thought you were going to establish your kingdom. I thought you were the son of God and now they've got you on a cross like a common criminal. What happened?* Peter was so disappointed in Jesus that the

Bible says he went back to fishing again. He was so discouraged with the people, so discouraged with Jesus, that he said, "Forget it. I'll go back and do what I know how to do."

When people disappoint us, we may want to give up. I've heard people say, "Oh, those people at the church really disappointed me," and not only do they leave the church, but they also turn their backs on the Lord.

We all disappoint each other. So how do we deal with that? When I feel like others have disappointed me, I first try to think, *How many people in my lifetime have I disappointed?* Probably more than I will ever know. I hate living up to people's expectations. So why should I make other people live up to my expectations of them?

Nowhere in the Bible does it say, "When people let you down, you are free to walk away from me and the church, thus saith the Lord." It's not there. But for some reason people will walk out on God just because they are disappointed by someone in the church.

If the Holy Spirit is indwelling me, then when somebody disappoints me, I have absolute power to forgive them. Everyone is going to disappoint us at one time or another. That's life. We need to keep our eyes focused on Jesus.

I have been like Epaphroditus. I've been sick overseas, and unable to finish the job I set out to do. I have also been part of a church that felt like someone let us down. I've been disappointed in myself.

You will face struggles and disappointments. You will stumble. Maybe you're already disappointed with yourself, with others, or in your circumstances. But no matter what it is, God is still at work. He cares more about relationships with his children than the things we consider "good" or "successful." God still accomplishes his purposes in us and through us, whether life is smooth sailing or stormy.

CHAPTER 14

REJOICE!

FINALLY, MY BROTHERS, REJOICE IN THE LORD! IT IS NO TROUBLE FOR ME TO WRITE THE SAME THINGS TO YOU AGAIN, AND IT IS A SAFEGUARD FOR YOU. WATCH OUT FOR THOSE DOGS, THOSE MEN WHO DO EVIL, THOSE MUTILATORS OF THE FLESH. FOR IT IS WE WHO ARE THE CIRCUMCISION, WE WHO WORSHIP BY THE SPIRIT OF GOD, WHO GLORY IN CHRIST JESUS, AND WHO PUT NO CONFIDENCE IN THE FLESH—THOUGH I MYSELF HAVE REASONS FOR SUCH CONFIDENCE. IF ANYONE ELSE THINKS HE HAS REASONS TO PUT CONFIDENCE IN THE FLESH, I HAVE MORE: CIRCUMCISED ON THE EIGHTH DAY, OF THE PEOPLE OF ISRAEL, OF THE TRIBE OF BENJAMIN, A HEBREW OF HEBREWS; IN REGARD TO THE LAW, A PHARISEE; AS FOR ZEAL, PERSECUTING THE CHURCH; AS FOR LEGALISTIC RIGHTEOUSNESS, FAULTLESS.

—PHILIPPIANS 3:1–6

One of the things I like about Pentecostal churches is the fact that many times in their services they will praise the Lord together. Somebody will say, "Let us praise the Lord together!" and everyone will start praising God out loud together at the same time. While people may be confused by all of the noise, God delights in hearing each voice. God listens to prayers all over the world, and he loves the praise of his people.

Paul says, "Rejoice in the Lord!" Why does he say this? Because he is getting ready to attack the law and some of the customs, so he takes a moment to remind them that they should rejoice in the Lord, not in traditions and legalism.

Paul is like a father caring for his children. In effect he is saying, "It's no big deal for me to bring these things up again because I love you so much." His instruction is, "Rejoice in the Lord." The word "rejoice" literally refers to verbally praising the Lord.

The problem was that some Gentiles were coming to Jesus, and the Jews told them that they had to take on Jewish customs as well. These Judaizers followed all the laws and customs of the Jews, while having faith in Jesus, and they wanted to force the same requirements on the new Gentile Christians.

The Real Issue

In Acts 15, Luke tells the story of Paul and Barnabas and the dispute that arose between them and the Judaizers. These people were infiltrating the church and trying to get the new converts to adopt the Jewish customs, making them feel less spiritual if they refused.

Circumcision was one of the big issues for these zealous Jews. They believed that true followers of Jesus must be circumcised according to the law given in Leviticus, as a sign of allegiance to the Lord. Even today, many cultures still practice ritual circumcision.

Paul's response isn't exactly calm and gentle. "Watch out for those dogs, those men who do evil, those mutilators of the flesh," he says. Instead of rejoicing in the Lord, these men were rejoicing in the law.

As you might surmise, calling someone a "dog" was not a sign of admiration. Paul was not thinking of the little puppies that come and crawl up in your lap. He's referring to scavengers, intimidators who ran around in packs, nipping at the heels of these new Christians, telling them, "You've got to do this and this and that ..."

Paul was concerned for the new converts, because he knew that if they were not grounded firmly in Christ, they would be picked off by these "dogs." Paul wanted to make sure that the new believers were growing in the knowledge of the Lord. It's interesting that so many times our discipleship is focused on those who've known the Lord a long time, instead of providing new Christians with strong fellowship groups. They are often the ones who most need encouragement and teaching.

Next Paul calls these Judaizers evildoers. They were clinging to their rules and regulations, and they considered themselves blameless. That's why Paul has to say, "Yeah, you keep the letter of the law. But look at my life. I have more reason to boast, yet I consider it rubbish."

Finally, he calls them "mutilators of the flesh." That's some pretty strong language. Paul really didn't want his Christian brothers at Philippi to be led astray by these false teachers.

Paul recognized the legalism of these men because he was a Pharisee. He once did the same things and kept the same laws that they were keeping. But he remembered Jesus' teaching—the real issue is in the heart, not the outward appearance. God says, "Man looks at the outward appearance, but the LORD looks at the heart" (1 Sam. 16:7).

For many years, when I was working for the Luis Palau organization, I had to wear a suit every day. I don't mind wearing a suit, but my natural choice is to wear jeans. I especially don't like to preach in a suit.

I once had the opportunity to be a guest preacher at another church. They had two morning services and an evening service, and when I asked what I should wear, they told me to wear a suit for the morning and I could wear whatever I wanted for the evening service. So I wore a suit in the morning, and when I preached that evening, I wore jeans.

After the evening service, several people came over to me

and asked, "What happened to you between this morning and tonight? You really kicked it up a notch!" I smiled and realized that when I had to preach in a suit I felt restricted, but when I wore jeans I was laid back and could be myself.

I got a note one time that said, "Dear pastor, thank you for wearing a suit this past Sunday. Now you look like our pastor." I laughed a little bit, and then I didn't wear a suit the next Sunday, just because I'm a rebel. If someone wants to wear a suit or a nice dress to church, that's great. Personally, I believe you can wear whatever you want.

People have always said, "You should wear your best to church because it's God's house and you need to show reverence for him." There is some truth to that, but I believe that Jesus is more concerned with the heart. He wore average-looking clothes. When he looked at the religious leaders who were wearing nice robes, he criticized them because they looked really good on the outside but there was something wrong with their hearts.

God doesn't care whether your clothes came from Nordstrom or K-Mart. The real issue is what's inside the heart. That's the point Paul is making to the Philippians. He doesn't want them caught up in the issue of circumcision, which is an outward thing. I could preach in a suit, or robes, or a T-shirt and jeans, but what really matters is what's in my heart. If I come walking in with a big Bible under my arm but I'm hiding some gross sins in my personal life, then I'm not honoring God at all.

God doesn't judge me based on what clothes I'm wearing. Will what I'm wearing really bring me closer to him? Probably not. God looks at my heart and at your heart to see whether or not we are really following him.

Worshipping in the Spirit

In contrast to those who put confidence in legalistic things such as circumcision, those who have no confidence in the flesh are the ones who worship in the Spirit of God. Here Paul is not referring to worship through song, but worship through service.

In Romans 12:1 Paul writes, "Therefore, I urge you, brothers, in view of God's mercy, to offer your bodies as living sacrifices, holy and pleasing to God—this is your spiritual act of worship." The word *body* does not merely refer to the external. The Greeks thought of the body as the cage of the soul, but the Hebrews thought of the body and soul as one. Paul is telling us to worship God with our whole being, both with our physical bodies and with our hearts.

I remember reading a story about one particular family who worked as missionaries and desperately needed a break from their work in Kentucky. So they decided to make the trip to visit family in Washington. Traveling in below-zero weather was especially difficult with a baby and an only partially working heater in the car.

Upon reaching Colorado, they had only a little bit of change left, so Ken pulled into a parking lot to discuss with Barbara what they should do about their critical financial situation. Barbara said, "We do what we preach. We believe the Lord and pray." They bowed their heads and asked the Lord to send help for them. When they finished praying, they drove to a service station and sat there wondering what was going to happen.

Another car pulled in behind them, and a lady got out and came up to their window. Very excitedly she remarked, "I saw you parked back by the grocery store with your heads bowed. I told my husband that I believed you were Christians and that you were praying for financial assistance. I want to help you." Reaching in the window, she placed money in their hands. Overwhelmed with the miracle they beheld, they thanked her and praised God for his provision.

That woman was walking in the Spirit. She worshipped by serving. We can have our rules and regulations and believe that they make us spiritual, but for her to see a couple with their heads bowed and realize that they needed money took the Spirit speaking to her. How are you at living in the Spirit?

I have twenty-five years worth of messages and sermon notes in the files in my office, and I would gladly speak again on most of the topics. However, there is one message that I do not remember with fondness. Back in high school, while attending a Christian school for a short time, I decided to sign up for a speech contest.

I didn't have time to prepare anything, so I got some notes that somebody at church had given me. It was an attack against "the Jesus people," a well-known Christian movement at the time. Of course, I had never met "the Jesus people." I had never even been to Los Angeles. I just had somebody else's thoughts, somebody else's accusations, and decided to attack "the Jesus people" in my speech. I did well on my speech and received a ribbon.

I am embarrassed to remember that day. Unfortunately, I wasn't walking in the Spirit. I didn't know a whole lot when I was sixteen years old. I didn't realize that "the Jesus people," with Chuck Smith, started Calvary Chapel. They aren't Pentecostal or even charismatic, but I love the focus they place on the Holy Spirit. It's a great reminder to me of what the apostle Paul is saying, that we should live in the Spirit.

Paul goes on to say that we glory in Christ, and put our confidence in him. The word *glory* means "to boast." We can boast about Jesus and what he has done for us. Paul could easily have boasted in himself, as you can see from his credentials and his accomplishments. But that isn't where he placed his confidence.

There's an old adage that says, "The Lord helps those who help themselves." We love to think that about the things we have done that make us feel good about ourselves. We want to show everyone how spiritual we are by what we have accomplished. Too often we place our confidence in the flesh.

Eugene Peterson writes, "Christian spirituality does not begin with us talking about our experience. It begins with listening to

God call us, heal us, and forgive us."[1] We are able to listen to God when we bow to the Spirit and do not bow to the flesh.

I have discovered in my Christian life that it is easier to obey laws than to build relationships. Have you ever noticed that? It would be easier if we could just keep the Ten Commandments and not worry about developing a relationship with the living Christ. Laws require no thinking. We just obey them, and then we can be proud in our ability to keep the law.

A relationship is different. It requires introspection, honesty, vulnerability, and brokenness. It requires us to be real and ask questions. Building a relationship with God takes time in worship and prayer. Yet that is what Christ is calling us to—a relationship where we truly experience him. It goes beyond my Sunday morning activities and permeates my whole life.

The law had a purpose and a reason—it showed us our need for a Savior. But we can rejoice that we are not bound by the traditions of men. We have freedom in Christ, freedom to walk in the Spirit and let his voice guide and direct our lives.

CHAPTER 15

NO COMPARISON

BUT WHATEVER WAS TO MY PROFIT I NOW CONSIDER LOSS FOR THE SAKE OF CHRIST. WHAT IS MORE, I CONSIDER EVERYTHING A LOSS COMPARED TO THE SURPASSING GREATNESS OF KNOWING CHRIST JESUS MY LORD, FOR WHOSE SAKE I HAVE LOST ALL THINGS. I CONSIDER THEM RUBBISH, THAT I MAY GAIN CHRIST AND BE FOUND IN HIM, NOT HAVING A RIGHTEOUSNESS OF MY OWN THAT COMES FROM THE LAW, BUT THAT WHICH IS THROUGH FAITH IN CHRIST—THE RIGHTEOUSNESS THAT COMES FROM GOD AND IS BY FAITH. I WANT TO KNOW CHRIST AND THE POWER OF HIS RESURRECTION AND THE FELLOWSHIP OF SHARING IN HIS SUFFERINGS, BECOMING LIKE HIM IN HIS DEATH, AND SO, SOMEHOW, TO ATTAIN TO THE RESURRECTION FROM THE DEAD.

—PHILIPPIANS 3:7–11

We compare all the time. We compare the old with the new; we compare our jobs, homes, possessions, and our families with other people. For some people, comparisons lead them to believe that the grass is always greener on the other side of the fence.

In this passage, Paul compares a few things. After instructing the Philippians to put no confidence in the flesh, he tells them where they should put their confidence—in knowing Christ and the power of his resurrection.

Paul knew that his credentials were only good for this world. All the notoriety, all the accolades, and all his accomplishments were present gains that were nothing when compared to knowing Christ. He considered them rubbish— literally "garbage."

I have seen ministers come to Christ. It is quite a shock to most people, but I have seen pastors of all backgrounds come forward at evangelistic events and pray to accept Christ. It might be hard for some of us to imagine. Some people are walking around like Paul was, trying to reach God by doing good deeds. Jesus finally came to Paul and showed him that he needed faith, because without it, nothing else matters.

G. K. Chesterton wrote, "Let your religion be less of a theory and more of a love affair."[1] As a Pharisee, Paul certainly had the theory down, but he had to realize that faith was more important in bringing him to the point of salvation.

Unfortunately, humans have always wanted to make up rules for God. The Pharisees had more than six hundred rules and regulations. Keeping them supposedly would make them spiritual and bring them closer to God. As Paul looks back, he realizes that all those laws didn't do a bit of good. They were all worthless compared to knowing Jesus.

We have to ask ourselves: Would I consider everything I have as garbage compared to knowing Christ? Is he all I need?

Knowing Christ versus Knowing About Christ

Paul knew who Christ was all along. He had persecuted the church dutifully and knew all about what they believed. He wanted to put them all in prison because he believed that their teachings were false. It took a personal encounter with Jesus to show him that knowing *about* Christ was not the same thing as truly knowing him.

Now, retrospectively, Paul says, "I wouldn't go back to that life, to all those rules and regulations and legalism. Keeping the law didn't give me peace in my heart. Now that I know Jesus, those things can't compare."

This word *know* that Paul uses does not mean simply having head knowledge. It means "to know experientially." Paul is referring to a personal, intimate relationship with the God of the universe. Before, he knew *about* Jesus—he could tell you where Jesus was born and what he taught. But now, he knew Jesus *experientially*, because he talked with him and listened to his voice.

Because we have the experience of this relationship, we can trust Jesus. When we go through difficulties, we can have confidence that Jesus is there because we have learned to truly know him.

In many places in America you can still wake up on a Sunday morning and find all of the stores and businesses closed because everyone goes to church. People have been doing it for years, because that's what their parents did, and their grandparents before them—it is culturally acceptable. They take their Bibles with them and pray prayers that have been passed down from generation to generation. From the outside, they look good.

However, when you really get to know these people, you realize that they may have gone to church all their lives, but some have never really known the transformation of having Jesus in their lives. They may be nice people, but they have never come to a point of truly understanding what it means to know Jesus Christ. Although they may be educated in Scripture, sometimes even the ministers have never committed their lives to the Lord.

Tertullian, one of the early church fathers, wrote, "A man becomes a Christian. He is not born one."[2] Sometimes that is hard to understand for people who have grown up in a culture where everyone goes to church because it is the socially acceptable thing to do. To them, being a Christian often means you have a Bible, you go to church, and you love America. They don't realize they need to admit they're sinners and believe in Jesus' death and resurrection.

Paul didn't want to be religious anymore. He didn't even necessarily want to be a Christian. He wanted to know Jesus. Paul had been a Pharisee. He knew the Pharisee's prayer: Lord, I thank you that I'm not like those sinners (Luke 18:11). That prayer didn't please God, though. What the Lord wanted to hear was the person who cried out, "Lord, be merciful to me, a sinner."

You could go to church every Sunday, and even be an elder or a deacon, but that alone won't transform you. Religion has no power to save or transform. Real power comes from a relationship with Jesus, who gives us the power to change and who transforms us to glorify him.

If you were to ask a newlywed couple, "Do you know each other?" I'm sure they would say, "Oh, yes." If you had asked me that question when I got married, I would have said, "Of course, we dated for three and a half years. I know her like the back of my hand." What newlywed couple doesn't feel that way?

I guarantee you that if you ask a couple who has been married for ten years, "Hey, back when you were first married, did you guys know each other very well?" they would say, "Hmm, not as well as we thought we did."

When we married, I thought I knew my wife, Deb, like the back of my hand. Ten years later, I realized that I didn't know her like the back of my hand. Twenty years later, I was trying to find the back of my hand. Fortunately, we continue to grow in the marriage relationship. Now, when Deb is speaking with other people, she often says something like, "No, I don't think Dan would go for that." Ninety percent of the time she's right, because she knows me pretty well after twenty-six years.

When it comes time to buy my wife a gift, I know her well enough that I get the right gift about fifty percent of the time. "What do you mean you don't want a Harley jacket for Christmas?" Well, I am still learning.

This is what Paul is talking about. As we spend time with Jesus, we get to know him better and we understand his goal and purposes.

How important is it for you right now to know Jesus better? Do you know Jesus better now than you did five years ago? The only way to know him better is to spend time every day in prayer and reading his Word. Not only do we talk to him in prayer, but we also listen to him and let him guide us and give us wisdom.

Resurrection Power versus Human Effort

In verse 10, Paul prays to know Christ and the power of his resurrection. He understood the importance of this power. He wanted to be strong and unwavering in his ministry. In order to do that, he needed the power that Jesus gives us.

In America, we have a great dependency on power sources. We just flip on a switch, and there's light. We open the refrigerator to get an ice cold drink. If we want something, we can usually just flip a switch or plug it in.

However, if you travel to another country like Uganda, you will find that you cannot depend on the power. One time I went to a little hotel restaurant in Uganda to get some lunch. The waiter gave me a menu, and I pointed to the first thing on it. He looked at me and said, "No power, no food." If you don't have any power, you can't cook.

"How long will it be off?" I asked.

"Don't know," was the response. I learned to bring food with me wherever I went from then on. In Uganda (and many other countries), the power comes on and goes off again without warning. They don't have a dependable supply of power or the money to be able to afford it all the time.

The New Testament is all about power—spiritual power. We have power to deal with sin and we have power over death. But power goes far beyond that. We have power to overcome ourselves, our weaknesses, and the things that we couldn't deal with otherwise. Jesus, through the Holy Spirit, gives us power to overcome. We overcome Satan by the power of Scripture.

Paul had human effort. He was a zealous Pharisee, found faultless according to the law. He had all that going for him, but it was nothing compared to the power of knowing Christ. He knew the power of being united with Christ in his resurrection (Rom. 6:5). However, he also knew that this power only comes when we have a right purpose and right motives. Otherwise, we are just striving in vain with our human efforts.

Suffering with Purpose versus Suffering without Hope

Paul understood that life would never be without suffering. So he asks to share in the fellowship of Christ's sufferings, because he knew that would be far better than suffering without any hope.

Sometimes when people pray for God to remove an affliction or trial from their lives, and it doesn't happen, they say, "See, God really doesn't have the power." But Paul doesn't shy away from suffering. He understands that it is part of the Christian experience.

That's something we normally don't tell people. We like to say, "Come to Jesus and everything will be wonderful." The truth is, when you come to Jesus, life can get really bad. For example, the early Christians endured ridicule, torture, and death as common, everyday occurrences. We suffer because of the evil that is all around us—random acts of violence.

We suffer because our bodies fail and break down. Sometimes, especially in other countries, believers suffer for standing up for Jesus. We suffer because life has both joys and sorrows and because we have an enemy prowling around like a lion, seeking to hurt us (1 Peter 5:8).

During my trip to Uganda, our group had the opportunity to walk through a camp of displaced persons. It was one of the saddest sights I have ever seen, looking into the eyes of thousands of men, women, and children displaced by rebel forces who came through killing everyone in their path. These people lived in tiny huts, eating one meal a day, unable to work because their land was taken away.

We hate suffering in America. In our mindset, we do everything we can to avoid suffering. The most horrible thing we can think about is death. We don't want to die. Before we left for Uganda, I looked in a travel guide and read this comment: "Going to Lira, Uganda, is suicidal."

I started thinking about that. "Okay, so what happens if I get killed?" It just means that I would arrive in heaven a little bit sooner than my family. I don't have a death wish, but we treat it like it's the worst thing in the world. However, Paul knew that suffering was part of being a Christian.

In Romans 8:18 Paul writes, "I consider that our present sufferings are not worth comparing with the glory that will be revealed in us."

Often the Lord allows suffering in our lives to grow us, to make us, and to mold us. Paul also knew that at the end of his life, he was going to die and the only thing that would matter was how he served Christ.

Rules and regulations are dead. They are all rubbish; they are completely worthless compared to knowing Jesus Christ our Lord. Nothing compares to truly experiencing God. Knowing him and the power of his resurrection makes even suffering worth it, because that draws us into a deeper relationship with him.

CHAPTER 16

THE RACE FOR THE PRIZE

*NOT THAT I HAVE ALREADY OBTAINED ALL THIS, OR HAVE
ALREADY BEEN MADE PERFECT, BUT I PRESS ON TO TAKE HOLD
OF THAT FOR WHICH CHRIST JESUS TOOK HOLD OF ME. BROTHERS,
I DO NOT CONSIDER MYSELF YET TO HAVE TAKEN HOLD OF IT.
BUT ONE THING I DO: FORGETTING WHAT IS BEHIND AND
STRAINING TOWARD WHAT IS AHEAD, I PRESS ON TOWARD THE
GOAL TO WIN THE PRIZE FOR WHICH GOD HAS CALLED ME
HEAVENWARD IN CHRIST JESUS. ALL OF US WHO ARE MATURE
SHOULD TAKE SUCH A VIEW OF THINGS. AND IF ON SOME POINT
YOU THINK DIFFERENTLY, THAT TOO GOD WILL MAKE CLEAR
TO YOU. ONLY LET US LIVE UP TO WHAT WE
HAVE ALREADY ATTAINED.*

—PHILIPPIANS 3:12–16

As the apostle Paul prepares to conclude his letter to the Philippians, I picture him with a big smile on his face. This is a book about joy. He is probably thinking of all the things he has left behind—the rules and regulations—and smiling as he describes what lies ahead of him.

I enjoy reading out of *The Message.* Of course, one must realize that it is a paraphrase, not a translation, but often it gives me a new way to look at a passage I've read many times before. Here's how Eugene Peterson puts Philippians 3:12–16:

I'm not saying that I have this all together, that I have it made. But I am well on my way, reaching out for Christ, who has so wondrously reached out for me. Friends, don't get me wrong: By no means do I count myself an expert in all of this, but I've got my eye on the goal, where God is beckoning us onward—to Jesus. I'm off and running, and I'm not turning back. So let's keep focused on that goal, those of us who want everything God has for us. If any of you have something else in mind, something less than total commitment, God will clear your blurred vision— you'll see it yet! Now that we're on the right track, let's stay on it.

Paul is saying, "I'm not going back." He uses an analogy he is quite fond of—a runner in a race. Because of his use of the first person, when he says, "I do not consider myself yet to have taken hold of it," and "I press on toward the goal to win the prize," we see Paul's tremendous humility. He knows he's not there yet.

Paul could have pontificated about all the great things he had done and how he had meticulously adhered to the law. That was the old Paul, the persecutor of the church. This is the new Paul, the Spirit-filled Paul, who knows the grace of God. He realizes that all those credentials and accomplishments are rubbish, and that what counts is the goal he is working toward—which he has not yet attained.

In ministry we have what we call "old school" preachers and "new school" preachers. An "old school" preacher is the preacher who continues to put himself above the congregation, using the terms "you" and "they" but never putting himself in the situation of the message or sermon. By his attitude he comes across sounding perfect, as if he never struggled with the sin he is preaching about.

In contrast, we have "new school" preachers, who use terms like "we" and "us," grouping themselves in with their congregations, relating to them even when it means admitting their struggles.

Sometimes "old school" preachers literally wipe out in ministry. They get so exhausted keeping up the pretense of being a perfect minister or a perfect minister's wife. They have to have perfect children who never do anything wrong, a perfect family that always has devotions together at 6:00 a.m. After a while, it gets tedious to maintain, and they burn out.

Paul gives us an example of what we ministers should be like. He admits, "I'm not there yet. I'm still growing and learning. Even though I see the prize laid out ahead of me, I'm still striving to know Jesus more." What an encouragement that is!

Although many early Christians probably wanted to put Paul on a pedestal because of all he had done, he says, "Don't put your eyes on me—put your eyes on Jesus." I pray that I am that way. We're all just normal people, striving for the same thing—to know and experience the resurrection power that Paul is talking about and to share in the suffering of Christ.

Sometimes it's hard to be transparent like Paul. In Romans 7:15, he says, "I do not understand what I do. For what I want to do I do not do, but what I hate I do." In all his writings, he is so open, always letting us see straight into his heart.

As Americans, we tend to struggle with being totally open and honest. In our small groups, with our brothers and sisters in Christ, if someone asks for a prayer request, we might say, "Oh, my car broke down." Many of us stay guarded in those situations. Instead, it would be so much better if we could have the transparency that Paul uses here and be able to say, "Yes, I'm hurting," or "I'm struggling, and I could really use prayer because I'm doubting my faith."

Remember, just as runners in a race, we are all in this race of the Christian life, trying to live in a way that is glorifying to God. Paul has some great advice for us along the way.

Avoid Distractions

Runners don't have time to look at what is behind them. They can't let the things going on around them be a distraction.

I am not a track and field fan, but I love to watch Marion Jones run. Her face lights up as she speeds past everyone. Imagine what would happen if she looked to the side and noticed one of the other women she was running against. "Oh, those are nice running shoes you have—nice color." Or what if she glanced over to the crowd, "Oh, hi, Mom and Dad, nice to see you." She wouldn't last. She can't let anything distract her, and she can't worry about what is going on behind her.

Paul looks back at his accomplishments, at all those things he held on to, and he says, "Forget it." He can forget what lies behind because the present is better, and he knows that the future will be even better than that.

Sometimes we like to talk of the "good old days." Are they really the good old days? If I know Jesus better than I did five years ago, then today is a much better day than five years ago. If I know Jesus better than I knew him ten years ago—and I am experiencing him in greater power and awareness—then today is the best day. I think that's the way Paul saw it.

Some of us have a hard time forgetting the past. The problem is that we have not yet learned to forgive. We push things to the back of our minds and we can't move forward because some issue is holding on to us.

I used to be a runner. About eight years ago, I would run four miles every day. If I tried to run now, I would probably have a heart attack within four feet. My knees would give out trying to carry my weight. It would be like running with a ball and chain around me.

Some Christians are carrying around a spiritual ball and chain, unable to run because they have resentment or bitterness tucked away inside of them. We need the transformation of the Holy Spirit to produce forgiveness in our souls and allow us to run freely as runners who aren't distracted by the world or our own sin.

Stay Focused

When the gun goes off and the runners take off down the track, you wouldn't see one of them pausing to look back at the starting blocks and say, "Wow, cool, look how far I've come! That's really great." They have to look ahead at where they are going.

I have read that if you use a cell phone while driving you are 35 percent more likely to get into a car accident. Why? Because it is a major distraction to most people to have to hold something and carry on a conversation while driving.

Sin in our lives is always a distraction until we deal with it. It blocks our desire and ability to know Jesus. Maybe you have experienced that feeling of being laden with guilt, feeling like the Lord is so far away. We let some sin creep into our lives and then Jesus feels like a stranger.

Someone has said that fools wander, but a wise man travels. In other words, the wise man has a goal in front of him. For Paul, that goal was to know Jesus. He knew that sin would distract him from pursuing this goal.

Do you set spiritual goals for your life? Most of us naturally have goals in our lives, whether it's to get wealthy, or to become successful in business, or to raise wonderful children. But how often do we set spiritual goals?

One goal might be to choose one day of the month to fast, not out of legalism, but an honest desire to spend time with Jesus. Instead of eating, you would spend that time in Bible study and prayer. Or you might decide that you want to learn something new about Jesus, and find a good book to study. Another great goal is to set a specific amount of time to spend in prayer—more than you ever have before.

A spiritual goal is something that you can measure to see whether you have actually been growing in your faith. Whether you set a goal to read one Christian book a month, or to give sacrificially out of your finances to someone in need, a goal will keep you focused on what lies ahead.

A good runner is not distracted by what's going on around him because his eyes are firmly focused on the goal. Paul said, "I press on toward the goal." It doesn't matter if your goal is far off or coming into view; what matters is that you are going after it with all of your heart.

Compete for the Prize

In 1 Corinthians 9:24, Paul writes, "Do you not know that in a race all the runners run, but only one gets the prize? Run in such a way as to get the prize." Paul wasn't running just to get to the finish line—he also knew that there was a prize waiting for him.

When I was running, my prize was being healthy and able to fit into some of my clothes again. Some runners run for money, or fame, or just for the thrill. Paul was running for the greatest prize of all—heaven, and the rewards he would receive from Jesus.

One of the couples on my board of directors for Eternity Minded Ministries continually amazes me with their generosity. They are fairly well off financially, but rather than spend their money on the comforts of this world, they give large amounts to the church and missions. They are committed to seeing people come to Christ, and because God has blessed them financially, they are able to make a huge impact in that way. I believe God will reward them for their generosity.

In Matthew 19, Jesus talks about rewards in the kingdom. In verse 29 he says, "Everyone who has left houses or brothers or sisters or father or mother or children or fields for my sake will receive a hundred times as much and will inherit eternal life." For every small contribution we make here on earth, we will receive a hundred times that much in rewards when we get to heaven!

C. S. Lewis said, "Aim at heaven and you will get earth thrown in. Aim at earth and you get neither."[1] Why do we stay committed to the race? Because we love the Lord? I hope that's part of our motivation. But deep inside, I think the idea of heaven and its rewards drives us on. Paul knew that his present life was rubbish compared to the prize for which God was calling him heavenward. He looked forward to being in the presence of the Lord.

Picture yourself running a race. As you make the final sprint, tearing through the ribbon, envision Jesus standing there with open arms, ready to say, "Well done, faithful servant." Jesus is waiting for you. Heaven is waiting for you. Run in such a way that you will obtain your prize.

CHAPTER 17

BALANCING ACT

JOIN WITH OTHERS IN FOLLOWING MY EXAMPLE, BROTHERS, AND TAKE NOTE OF THOSE WHO LIVE ACCORDING TO THE PATTERN WE GAVE YOU. FOR, AS I HAVE OFTEN TOLD YOU BEFORE AND NOW SAY AGAIN EVEN WITH TEARS, MANY LIVE AS ENEMIES OF THE CROSS OF CHRIST. THEIR DESTINY IS DESTRUCTION, THEIR GOD IS THEIR STOMACH, AND THEIR GLORY IS IN THEIR SHAME. THEIR MIND IS ON EARTHLY THINGS. BUT OUR CITIZENSHIP IS IN HEAVEN. AND WE EAGERLY AWAIT A SAVIOR FROM THERE, THE LORD JESUS CHRIST, WHO, BY THE POWER THAT ENABLES HIM TO BRING EVERYTHING UNDER HIS CONTROL, WILL TRANSFORM OUR LOWLY BODIES SO THAT THEY WILL BE LIKE HIS GLORIOUS BODY.

—PHILIPPIANS 3:17–21

When I was young, my parents bought a house in a neighborhood that had not yet been fully developed, so we had lots of room to go exploring. My friends and I would take shortcuts across the fields and through walnut orchards—usually cutting through someone's backyard. Occasionally we would run into a problem—a wooden fence. So my buddies would jump up on top of the railing and walk across the fence. Unfortunately, I never had a good sense of balance, so I would end up scooting along on my backside behind them.

Sometimes I feel that life is like that. Instead of having everything in order, we end up scooting along on our backsides, unable to balance the way our friends seem to be able to. A magazine article I read said that only 2 percent of Americans feel like their lives are balanced.

Earlier in chapter 3, Paul dealt with the issue of people whose lives were not balanced—the Judaizers. These legalists put all the weight on their old traditions. Paul rebuked them because they ignored the grace of God. Now, he has to deal with the other side of the spectrum—Libertines. These people professed to be Christians, yet their lives displayed an indulgence of earthly pleasures. They, too, ignored the grace of God.

Paul uses some pretty strong language when he calls them "enemies of the cross of Christ." In Romans 16:17–18 he further describes them, saying, "I urge you, brothers, to watch out for those who cause divisions and put obstacles in your way that are contrary to the teaching you have learned. Keep away from them. For such people are not serving our Lord Christ, but their own appetites. By smooth talk and flattery they deceive the minds of naive people."

Such people set their minds on earthly things. In contrast, Paul was focusing on the future and his heavenly prize. The apostle John wrote, "Do not love the world or anything in the world" (1 John 2:15). Instead of following after Christ, the Libertines were living for the world and its empty possessions.

Paul urges believers to find a balance between being a Judaizer and a Libertine. Neither group displayed the character of Jesus. Something had gone wrong—their lives had not been transformed. They were continuing to live the way they had lived before they decided to follow Christ. Paul is saying, "Don't go down either of these roads. Be balanced. Imitate me in the way I follow Jesus."

Paul invites us to follow his example. He's not saying it egotistically, "Look, I'm better than everybody. Follow me." He has already said that he's not there yet, that he hasn't obtained this righteousness, but he has a passion to follow Jesus and he wants these Christians to share that passion.

The New Testament had not yet been completed at this time. The Philippian believers couldn't just pick up their Bibles and read about Jesus and how he lived. So Paul offers himself as an example for them to follow.

The old line "Do what I say, not what I do" doesn't work out very well because we learn by example. We like to mimic what we see in people we respect, those who are our leaders.

Are our lives balanced enough that we could say to someone, "Listen, I'm not perfect, but you can imitate me because I am following Christ with all my heart"?

Defining a Balanced Life

If I only miss church two Sundays a year, or pray a certain amount of time each day, will that give me a balanced Christian life? Of course not. Paul is talking about right motives, priorities, and goals. This doesn't mean we can't have fun. I would hate to give up motorcycling! A balanced person is able to put proper emphasis on all the different areas of life.

Few people wake up in the morning and think, "Lord, I'm going to go to work and serve you today." Normally our attitude goes something like, "I can't stand my boss and I'm sick of this job. I've got to find something else." Instead, what if we viewed our jobs in light of how we could use them to witness, or to earn money that we can use to further God's kingdom around the world?

Are we balanced in our Christian lives? Do we overemphasize one thing and yet not emphasize another area? Someone has said that being a balanced Christian is where the sacred and the secular blend together. You don't have to think, "Okay, I'm going to go to church this Sunday and I'm going to be with God," because you are thinking about being with God throughout your week.

Being balanced in the Christian life means that we know we are loved, but understand that we need forgiveness. We must know our strengths, yet be able to admit our weaknesses. Jesus helps us understand the balance of who we are in the world.

The Need for Balance

My friend Nigel visited from England, and we took him to San Francisco because he had never seen the city before. After crossing the Golden Gate Bridge, we stopped at a lookout point. It was extremely windy as we got out of the car, and as Nigel and I headed for the lookout, I heard my wife yelling at me, "Dan, I can't shut the door!" I walked over to inspect it and discovered that the latch wouldn't receive the bolt. I went over to the other door to see how it was designed, and noticed a little switch there. I flipped it. Unfortunately, when I tried to shut this door, it wouldn't latch either.

I got out the owner's manual, but even with my glasses on I couldn't figure it out! So Nigel and I had to sit in the back and hold the two back doors shut while Deb drove home. We had been going for several minutes when I realized that as long as the car was moving forward, I didn't need to hold the door. The force of the wind would keep it shut. It was a neat little trick until Deb slowed down, and the door went flying open.

Sometimes we get going so fast in life, and the wind is rushing by with so much force, that we find it hard to let the Lord in. We can't get the door open. But when we stop for a moment and meditate and reflect on who God is, our lives fall into balance. We let him in, and he brings our lives back to order.

Sometimes when I am in a group praying, it gets quiet and nobody prays for a while. As we sit there in silence, I like to contemplate on God and his holiness. When you focus on him, and realize that he is very aware of your situation, you become centered and balanced in him.

A. W. Tozer writes, "A real Christian is an odd number anyway. He feels supreme love for One whom he has never seen, talks familiarly every day to Someone he cannot see, expects to go to heaven on the virtue of Another, empties himself in order to be full, admits he is wrong so that he can be declared right, falls down in order to get up, is strongest when he is weakest, richest when he is poorest, and happiest when he feels worst. He dies so he can live, forsakes in order to have, gives away so he can keep, sees the invisible, hears the inaudible, and knows that which passes knowledge."[1] The only way for us to be truly balanced is by following in the footsteps of Jesus.

The Reason for Balance

Why don't we go the legalistic route and put more emphasis on our works and the good things we do? Or why don't we go to the other extreme and say, "Don't worry about it. I'm a Christian so I can enjoy all this sin. God will forgive me." The reason we need to be balanced, Paul explains, is that we are waiting for Jesus' return. That thought should have a major impact on our lives.

"Our citizenship is in heaven," Paul says in verse 20. Philippi was a Roman colony. They were proud to be associated with Rome, because even though they were just an outpost, they had all the privileges and rights as if they were living in the city of Rome itself. However, Paul wanted to remind believers that they had a new citizenship—a better citizenship—because they were now a colony of heaven. They had something great to look forward to.

John writes these powerful words about the return of Jesus. "And now, dear children, continue in him, so that when he appears we may be confident and unashamed before him at his coming" (1 John 2:28). What an awkward and embarrassing moment it would be if we had to hide in the corner at Christ's return because of the way we lived.

Are you living a balanced Christian life right now? If Jesus came back today, would you be ashamed to stand before him

because you have either been legalistic or lazy in your relationship with him?

I recently read a great story about Thomas Hamill, who
escaped from his captivity in Iraq. His wife and children had
received word from the captors that they were going to torture
and kill him, and they had been taunted by that news for three
weeks. When his wife, Kelly, received the phone call that her
husband had been found alive, she was overjoyed. I can just
imagine the excitement she must have shown as she flew to
Germany to meet him, eagerly anticipating his arrival.

Do we eagerly await Christ's return? Are we too busy keeping a long list of rules, or are we filling our lives with
worldliness? Are we letting life rush by us so fast that the door
is stuck and we can't let him in? He's coming back any day, and
I don't want to be embarrassed and shrink back when he
arrives.

God has given us the Holy Spirit to help keep us balanced,
to tap us on the shoulder and remind us when we're leaning too
far to one side, or when we're going too fast and need to slow
down and let God in. Is he prompting you to make some adjust-
ments in order to live a more balanced Christian life?

Chapter 18

United We Stand

Therefore, my brothers, you whom I love and long for, my joy and crown, that is how you should stand firm in the Lord, dear friends! I plead with Euodia and I plead with Syntyche to agree with each other in the Lord. Yes, and I ask you, loyal yokefellow, help these women who have contended at my side in the cause of the gospel, along with Clement and the rest of my fellow workers, whose names are in the book of life.

—*Philippians 4:1–3*

During a difficult time at the beginning of our country's history, founding father Benjamin Franklin said, "We must all hang together, or assuredly we shall all hang separately."[1] Martin Luther King Jr. said, "We may have all come on different ships, but we're in the same boat now."[2] Abraham Lincoln said the now famous phrase, "United we stand; divided we fall." Throughout America's history, unity has been an important concept.

In the Bible, unity refers to a sense of oneness. Jesus expected unity among his followers, and he prayed in John 17:23, "May they be brought to complete unity to let the world know that you sent me and have loved them even as you have loved me." Unfortunately, conflict sometimes destroys our unity, especially in the local church.

I've heard people say, "I don't want to go to church because people don't get along with each other and I don't want to get hurt." Sadly, in many cases that is true. Paul has been writing about joy, and he's getting ready to give some encouragement, but first he must deal with a problem of disunity in the church. Two women, Euodia and Syntyche, were having a conflict. Apparently this problem was big enough that Paul singled them out as he begins the final portion of his letter. He urges their fellow believers to help them in resolving the problem.

How do we resolve disunity within the body of Christ? I want to offer you a few principles from Scripture on how to deal with conflict in the church.

Don't Run

In verse 1, Paul says, "Stand firm in the Lord." Running away from conflict will not resolve it. We need to realize that conflict is part of life—whether you see it in the office, at home, or at a Bible study.

Because of our different personalities and backgrounds, we can expect conflict in life. You might have two kids who are so different from each other that they are always fighting. Or maybe there's a conflict in your neighborhood, and you have to hold meetings with your neighbors to discuss how to resolve it. Relatives can cause conflict quite frequently—especially the in-laws. What about team sports? There's a hotbed for conflict.

Paul's answer is, "Stand firm." This applies to several things he has been talking about. As we go through suffering, we can stand firm, knowing that we have the hope of heaven. Now, through this dissension, Paul uses the phrase because he knows that running away is not the answer.

Most people do not wake up in the morning and say, "Ah, I can hardly wait for some conflict to happen today." Although some people seem to enjoy conflict, most of us would rather turn and walk—or run—away from it. When Paul says, "Stand firm," he doesn't mean, "Don't do anything." He uses the same phrase in Ephesians 6:14, where he is talking about being prepared. Conflicts *will* arise, and if we have been allowing God to mold us through his Word, we will be prepared to handle them, standing firm—united in the truth.

Don't Sweep It

Another common response to conflict is to try to pretend it's not a big deal, or sweep it under the carpet. However, Paul realizes that this type of problem won't resolve itself—and he gets right down to naming names. He isn't being mean-spirited, but he realizes that he must confront these two women and call them specifically by name in order to deal with the issue properly. He does it out of the true love and concern that we saw in the first verse.

We don't really know a lot about this problem. However, we understand that these women were leaders in the church, and many believers looked up to them. Some scholars believe that one was of Jewish background and the other of Gentile, or Greek, background. Syntyche's name has origins in the pagan goddess of fortune. With different backgrounds, different nationalities, and maybe different socioeconomic backgrounds, they probably had different viewpoints on several occasions. Instead of working together in love, perhaps they both wanted to be in control.

Paul counts these women among his "fellow workers" (v. 3). They were in ministry with him, and because of that, Paul knew they would continue to cause problems if the conflict was pushed aside instead of worked out.

My friend Dr. Daniel Borg is a pastor and a professor who teaches in the areas of conflict resolution and conflict management. One time at a seminar, he gave a talk on the anatomy of a disagreement. At least three parties are involved, he said. First, there are the primaries. They are the ones who started the conflict and who are actively and personally involved.

Then there are the secondaries. These people side with the primaries, either because they believe in the point or because they are trying to be loyal to a friend. Have you ever been in that position? Maybe you have been pulled into a situation that started with just a couple of people and ended up involving half the church.

Finally, you have the innocent bystanders who are often affected by the conflict or the outcome of the conflict. Many Christians have been in that position.

As Paul writes this warning, he realizes that it is not only Euodia and Syntyche who are involved. This conflict will spread and affect the secondaries as well as some innocent bystanders. The health of a church, just like the health of a business organization, can rise and fall on one conflict that is allowed to grow instead of being dealt with. Jesus warned, "Every kingdom divided against itself will be ruined, and every city or household divided against itself will not stand" (Matt. 12:25).

In my own life, I have been in each situation. At times, sadly, I have been one of the primaries in a conflict. I have certainly been a secondary because I've often found myself in a leadership role and having to deal with the conflicts. Occasionally, I have been one of the innocent parties and have suffered the fallout of the problem.

Paul says, "Let's get this out in the open and deal with it." The consequences are always worse when the issue is swept under the carpet and we try to pretend that it's not really an issue.

Don't Ignore It

When we realize and admit that there is a problem, we can't ignore it. Paul was so concerned about this conflict that he asks others in the church to mediate. They could not resolve it themselves, and they needed help. In these cases, someone else needs to get involved—not a busybody, but someone who truly desires to bring the two people or groups together for the glory of God.

Jesus gave us some clear principles about dealing with conflict. In Matthew 5:23–24, he says, "Therefore, if you are offering your gift at the altar and there remember that your brother has something against you, leave your gift there in front of the altar. First go and be reconciled to your brother; then come and offer your gift." Ignoring the issue is not an option.

If you are on the other side of the situation, and have been the one wronged by another Christian, Jesus says, "If your brother sins against you, go and show him his fault, just between the two of you. If he listens to you, you have won your brother over" (Matt. 18:15). Later in the passage, Jesus lays out the rest of the plan if the person does not repent.

Another position you may have found yourself in is the mediator. In Acts 15, the church elders appointed two men to act as mediators in resolving a conflict between the Judaizers and Paul and Barnabas.

Unfortunately, many people do not want reconciliation. They don't want to forgive, because they would rather hold on to their hurt. Even though they may say, "Yes, I forgive you," to the other person, they still harbor hard feelings, and they still talk among their friends—their secondaries—about how they have been hurt.

It seems we like to wallow in our misery sometimes. We don't want to forgive because we feel that we have been injured too deeply. However, when we hold on to bitterness we literally give the enemy the right to come into our lives and take possession of what we do and who we are.

Paul understood the need to deal with this problem quickly so as not to give the devil a foothold. He writes in Ephesians 4:25–26, "Therefore each of you must put off falsehood and speak truthfully to his neighbor, for we are all members of one body. 'In your anger do not sin': Do not let the sun go down while you are still angry, and do not give the devil a foothold." Our adversary loves to use disunity in the church to break up congregations and put a wedge between brothers and sisters so that we are less effective witnesses to the world.

Another thing Paul was concerned about was the fact that, because of this conflict, the gospel would not move forward. Because Euodia and Syntyche were so caught up in their disagreement, they couldn't focus their attention on serving Jesus and sharing the good news.

When we are so wrapped up in the conflict within our churches, we aren't able to pour our energy into sharing Jesus with anyone. We talk about how God is going to judge the immoral and the sinners, but I'm concerned about how God will judge the churches in America. Many of them can't even think about the lost because they are so absorbed with the little disagreements that arise within the community of believers.

Paul knew what could happen to the Philippians if they ignored the conflict between these two women. It could continue to grow and become a distraction for them, keeping them from serving the Lord.

I have a friend who is the pastor of an American Baptist church on the East coast. He had been asking me to come talk about evangelism to his congregation. However, as he began to tell me about his church, I realized that my talk on reaching the lost wouldn't do any good. There was so much disunity in the church that they were not going to get anywhere until there was a renewal and an attitude of forgiveness to work through the conflicts and create a spirit of unity.

I recently received an e-mail from this pastor. He wrote, "They ran off my associate pastor this time. I'm so tired of the conflict at this church. All I deal with is conflict. We don't even do anything for the Lord anymore. I'm resigning." He

finally recognized that the clashes within the body of believers were keeping them from producing any real fruit for the
Lord.

Paul saw that his beloved church had to choose a direction. Either these women needed to deal with their conflict
and forgive each other, or they were going to continue to
build up their secondaries and drag others into the problem,
and end up causing a split in the church.

God has called us to be unified. The church should not be
a place of bickering and fighting, but a place where lives are
transformed, and where we see the Spirit of God at work.

Chapter 19

Joy in Prayer

Rejoice in the Lord always. I will say it again: Rejoice! Let your gentleness be evident to all. The Lord is near. Do not be anxious about anything, but in everything, by prayer and petition, with thanksgiving, present your requests to God. And the peace of God, which transcends all understanding, will guard your hearts and your minds in Christ Jesus.

—*Philippians 4:4–7*

One summer when I was a youth pastor, we took a group of high school students to a lake in the Sierra Mountains. The lake had a pontoon dock in the middle of it, so one of the other adults joined me in rowing out to reach the dock. We were fully dressed and didn't have our swimsuits on. Once we reached our destination, we tied up the boat and jumped onto the floating dock.

As soon as our feet hit the boards, we noticed something. There was a little hole in the middle of the dock, and out of it came hundreds of buzzing yellow jackets, disturbed from their slumber. I got stung eight or nine times before I could even hit the water. Without thinking about our clothes, we jumped in the water and literally swam the boat back to shore. We couldn't even get in the boat because the bees were everywhere.

Bees really make you move, as we found out. How many people have been in accidents because they were swatting at a bee inside the car? One little bee that could easily be squished will make a person go crazy. Some people are allergic to bee stings, so they have an excuse, but I don't know about the rest of us. Bees certainly get you moving.

In this passage we have a beehive of imperatives that Paul gives us to live by. They should get us moving as well. These verbs are in the imperative tense, which means that they are commands or obligatory duties. Your boss might say, "It is imperative for you to be at work by 7:00 a.m. so you don't lose your job." Here Paul is saying, "It is imperative that you do these things so that you can experience the peace of God."

The Message paraphrase by Eugene Peterson says: "Celebrate God all day, every day. I mean, revel in him! Make it as clear as you can to all you meet that you're on their side, working with them and not against them. Help them see that the Master is about to arrive. He could show up any minute! Don't fret or worry. Instead of worrying, pray. Let petitions and praises shape your worries into prayers, letting God know your concerns. Before you know it, a sense of God's wholeness, everything coming together for good, will come and settle you down. It's wonderful what happens when Christ displaces worry at the center of your life."

Be Joyful

Paul gives his first imperative twice: "Rejoice in the Lord always. I will say it again: Rejoice!" This is a present active imperative, which means "do it right now!" Right now, even in the midst of suffering, in the midst of the disunity in the church because of the conflict between Euodia and Syntyche, Paul wants the Philippians to rejoice.

We have all had situations in our lives when we have found it difficult to be joyful. When we experience disappointment, when people hurt us, or when our lives are full of trials or grief, we don't really feel like rejoicing.

One of the things we need to do in the midst of difficult situations is look for God. Do you see him in the suffering you are going through? Do you understand what he's trying to accomplish in and through your life? Is God making you stronger?

A seventeenth-century preacher named Jeremiah Burroughs wrote an incredible book called *The Rare Jewel of Christian Contentment.* In it he explains why believers should be filled with joy no matter what their circumstances are. He gives a few reasons why Christians should be content and not have a complaining spirit.[1]

First, complaining is a particularly serious offense in light of how we have been so greatly blessed—especially when we complain about trivial things.

I was standing in line at the bank, and the man behind me started complaining about the bank and the long line. He continued on in such a loud voice that he soon drew others into the conversation. After listening for a while, I turned around and said, "Listen, this bank is open six days a week. In some countries, the bank is only open one day a week, if that. Our money is insured by the federal government—we know it's worth the same this week as it was last week. There are plenty of countries where the government steals your money whenever they want to. I think we're pretty fortunate."

Second, Burroughs says that complaining is especially serious when done by those to whom God has been so gracious, because our troubles are often a part of God's plan to humble us.

Joy is the mark of the Holy Spirit in our lives. It convicts me even to write that. Yet I believe that joy is not based on temperament, personality, or feelings, but on how we let the indwelling Holy Spirit control our lives.

In times past, we were taught that Christians should be solemn. You may have been raised in that way. In the past, Christians walked into church without any laughing or greeting each other, sat down, and quietly listened to ministers who would not even smile from the pulpit because it was God's house.

In parts of that, we were on the right track. God is holy, and we should revere and respect him. However, we sometimes treat the physical house better than we treat our own bodies. Scripture says that our bodies are the temples of the Holy Spirit (1 Cor. 6:19). He lives inside of us, not in a building made by man.

Do we shine the truth joyfully in our lives? Do we rejoice in the Lord during difficult times because we know God is at work in us? Paul could say "rejoice"—even from prison.

Be Gentle

The Romans didn't like the word *gentle* any more than they liked the word *humble*. It symbolized weakness and frailty.

Paul says that our gentleness should be evident to everyone. The older I get, the harder I find it is to be gentle and patient—especially when I'm out on the freeway. There's always that person sitting in the fast lane doing the speed limit, backing up traffic for three miles. I find myself getting irritated at that point.

Jesus was the ultimate example of this attribute. First Peter 2:23 says, "When they hurled their insults at him, he did not retaliate; when he suffered, he made no threats." The prophet Isaiah tells us that Jesus allowed himself to be led like a lamb to the slaughter (53:7).

I was in a restaurant with a couple of other men. As we sat conversing, a young woman with a physical handicap walked up to our table. She was trying to sell us something. Some of the guys at our table began questioning her and making fun of her. I watched as she answered their questions and was gracious to them.

Her gentleness convicted me, so I took a closer look at what she was selling. She had made little placards with sayings on them, and one read, "People are lonely because they build walls instead of bridges." It looked interesting, so I said, "I'll take three of these." I took out my wallet and gave her some money, and she thanked me and left.

The following Sunday I was preaching at my church, and I looked down and there in the front row sat the same young woman. She smiled at me and I smiled back. I was struck with the realization that if I had been rude to her and said mean things, I would have been feeling pretty bad about myself right then. Thankfully, the Holy Spirit had prompted me to respond with gentleness.

Being gentle means that we yield our personal rights for the consideration of others. Paul also says to be gentle because the Lord could return at any time.

Don't Worry

Worrying is my "spiritual gift." My wife could tell you, I love to worry. This passage is especially challenging to me. The word *worry* means undue concern. It doesn't mean we shouldn't prepare and plan for events in life. This is directed at the person who continues to think over and rehash their circumstances, driving himself or herself deeper into despair.

Jesus instructed his disciples about worry. "Therefore I tell you, do not worry about your life, what you will eat or drink; or about your body, what you will wear. Is not life more important than food, and the body more important than clothes? Look at the birds of the air; they do not sow or reap or store away in barns, and yet your heavenly Father feeds them. Are you not much more valuable than they? Who of you by worrying can add a single hour to his life?" (Matt. 6:25–27).

Constant fear, apprehension, and worry are marks of an unbeliever. Paul is saying, "Knock it off. Stop worrying." How do we stop worrying? Paul's answer is by prayer. He doesn't say, "read your Bible," or "read a book about prayer." We have to really commune with the living God.

Paul uses three different words in this verse: *prayer, petition,* and *request. Prayer* denotes the person's heart attitude of worship. In difficult times, we should continue to worship and praise God for who he is.

Petition and *request* refer to expressing a need or desire. It might be, "Lord, I need you to help me through this difficult time," or "God, will you provide this for me?" When Paul says, "Present your requests to God," he uses the word that means "unreserved confidence." We don't have to keep anything back—we just need to tell God what is on our hearts.

Be Thankful

The attitude of Paul, and the attitude that we should have, is one of thanksgiving to God because he is the Creator and we are his creation. If you're a parent, you understand how nice it is to hear the words "thank you" from your kids.

Someone has said, "A single grateful thought raised to heaven is the most perfect prayer."[2] King David wrote, "How good it is to sing praises to our God, how pleasant and fitting to praise him!" (Ps. 147:1). C. S. Lewis had the right idea when he said, "We ought to give thanks for all fortune: if it is 'good,' because it is good, if it is 'bad,' because it works in us patience, humility, and contempt of this world and the hope of our eternal country."[3] Are we grateful people?

The Result

"And the peace of God, which transcends all understanding, will guard your hearts and your minds in Christ Jesus" (v. 7). We all want peace—peace in our hearts, in our homes, in our country. Here, Paul points out that peace comes as a consequence of our prayer life, when we habitually lay our concerns and worries at Jesus' feet.

True peace does not come from inside us. At times I have claimed to be at peace about a decision or situation that I had not really prayed about. It was just something I really wanted, so I convinced myself that God had given me that peace. If you are not walking with the Lord, and you say, "I have peace about this," that peace is not from God. It is your own will selfishly taking over your thoughts and feelings.

No amount of money can bring you this peace. God is bigger than your 401(k). He's bigger than the Social Security department. Your status in life or your accomplishments can't give you the peace that God offers.

This peace is a gift that God gives when we have a worshipping heart, when we have a heart that is dedicated to him, and when we ask him for guidance, healing, and strength. It stems from a regular prayer life in which we bring our will in line with God's perfect plan.

So how much prayer does it take? That's between you and your Father. But I can tell you it's more than just Sunday mornings or a quick "thanks" before a meal. When we truly have this peace—this divine peace, beyond all comprehension, that surpasses every human reason—we can go through the darkest nights and the deepest valleys without fear. The word *guard* is a military term, meaning that this peace will guard or keep out those thoughts and emotions that cause worry and anxiety.

There is no formula. There is no book that we can read or class that we can take. Only God can teach us to be people of prayer and give us that incredible joy, knowing that all of our cares and worries are in his capable hands.

CHAPTER 20

JOYFUL THOUGHTS

FINALLY, BROTHERS, WHATEVER IS TRUE, WHATEVER IS NOBLE, WHATEVER IS RIGHT, WHATEVER IS PURE, WHATEVER IS LOVELY, WHATEVER IS ADMIRABLE—IF ANYTHING IS EXCELLENT OR PRAISEWORTHY—THINK ABOUT SUCH THINGS. WHATEVER YOU HAVE LEARNED OR RECEIVED OR HEARD FROM ME, OR SEEN IN ME—PUT IT INTO PRACTICE. AND THE GOD OF PEACE WILL BE WITH YOU.

—PHILIPPIANS 4:8–9

One research team found that women speak around twenty-five thousand words each day, while men only use about twelve thousand. Presuming we speak even half of the things that go through our heads, that means we have thousands and thousands of thoughts each day. Although my wife may have more thoughts going through her head than I do, each one of us has thousands of thoughts and ideas competing for our attention.

In this passage, Paul wants us to realize that we choose what we think about. If we don't control those thoughts, they will soon control us. The peace he talks about will guard our hearts and our minds, but we have a responsibility to control what we allow our thoughts to dwell on. When we're faced with a problem or dilemma, our reaction is often based on how our thoughts are going—our self-talk. If we have a negative self-talk and we dwell on thoughts that are critical and gloomy, we will end up responding to life in that way. Our self-talk dictates the way we see life.

Paul understood the importance of our minds and our thoughts. In Romans he writes, "Do not conform any longer to the pattern of this world, but be transformed by the renewing of your mind. Then you will be able to test and approve what God's will is—his good, pleasing and perfect will" (12:2). Then in 2 Corinthians 10:5 he says, "We demolish arguments and every pretension that sets itself up against the knowledge of God, and we take captive every thought to make it obedient to Christ."

As Christians, we cannot simply let our thoughts go wherever they want to. If you let an angry or negative thought come into your mind, and you dwell on it long enough, it will eventually come out in a very ugly way. So Paul is saying take those thoughts captive, renew your mind, and bring your thought life under the control of Christ.

Jesus taught his disciples that sin begins in the mind. James tells us that sin can start out as a small desire—a mere thought. Our thoughts reveal who we really are. Proverbs 23:7 says, "For as he thinks in his heart, so is he" (NKJV). Paul's exhortation here is for us to consider carefully what we allow our thoughts to dwell on.

Paul uses several adjectives to describe what we should be thinking about. First, he says to think about things that are "true" and "noble," referring to the way we should live and speak—with an attitude of respect. "Right" and "pure" refer to those things that are right by the standards of God's holiness, not by the world's standards.

The two adjectives I want to focus on are the last two in Paul's list: "lovely" and "admirable." These are the ones that really spoke to my heart, and I pray they will speak to yours as well.

Whatever Is Lovely

You wouldn't normally hear me saying to my wife, "Oh, that's a lovely dress you have," or "That's a lovely motorcycle."

The word *lovely* is not a frequent one in my vocabulary. But here I find it refreshing.

Lovely is only used this one time in the New Testament, and it refers to something that a person has a friendly disposition toward. *The New Jerusalem Bible* translates the word with the phrase "everything we love." This is not a word about morality, like "pure" and "true," but it conveys the thought that we can appreciate what is good, such as things within our culture.

This comes back to the idea of being in this world but not of it. Can we enjoy life in America and still have a relationship with Christ? I believe that part of what Paul is saying here is that we can enjoy our culture and still be a strong follower of Jesus.

Jesus did not live as a hermit. Although he took time away to pray, he also embraced the Jewish culture. Most of his life, he lived as a regular Jew would live. He went to the weddings, parties, and family gatherings. He was a blue-collar worker. He wore the clothes of his day, observed the holidays, and ate the proper foods.

In Luke 15, Jesus teaches the story of the prodigal son by relating it directly to their culture. The Jews understood the significance of the ceremonial robe and the ring that the father gave his son. They knew what it meant to kill the fattened calf, which was only done on special occasions and holidays because they didn't eat meat on a regular basis.

Jesus related to the Jews because he understood their culture. He took what was good—what was lovely—and used it to teach them. As Christians, we should take from our culture what is morally good, what is enjoyable and loveable, and allow ourselves to think about those things.

Some Christians wake up in the morning with scowls on their faces. They view the world as completely evil, and they won't talk to any unbelievers because they don't want to become tainted. That's not what Jesus taught, and that's not what Paul is talking about. While we should be sensitive to evil, we can still enjoy the good things about being Americans—Fourth of July celebrations, weddings, parties, music, baseball, and apple pie. My wife's list might be a little different—shopping, nice restaurants, arts and crafts, and bonbons.

The key is to be discerning, as we learned in Philippians 1:10. We can enjoy our culture and the life we have, but we must be careful not to be captivated by the things of this world.

When I came to the Lord as a teenager, my church had many rules and regulations. It seemed like the only thing that a Christian was allowed to do for fun was to go to a potluck once a month. Then when I went to college, I had to sign a paper that said I would not do certain things. Life was presented as a trial we must go through, and as Christians, we couldn't really enjoy it.

I think Jesus had a great time here on earth. Even though he had the cloud of the cross above him all the time, I think he enjoyed things like spending time with his family, learning to work with wood, and helping others. In John 10:10, Jesus said, "I have come that they may have life, and have it to the full." He didn't say, "You give me your life, and I am going to make your life miserable."

Someone has written, "I asked God for all things that I might enjoy life. He gave me life so that I might enjoy all things."

Whatever Is Admirable

Again, this word *admirable* is found only here in the New Testament. It means "praiseworthy" or "attractive"—something that people appreciate. Some people appreciate a Beethoven symphony, or a colorful sunset. Most of us appreciate it when someone sacrifices for another person. As Christians, we should appreciate the good gifts that God gives us.

I'm not sure if there's anyone on this earth who enjoys life more and worries less than my wife. Every day is beautiful to her. For years I have watched Deb create things, find new projects, and enjoy collecting knickknacks. I'm sure God appreciates those things about her more than I do because he created her that way. I don't seem to have the same interests. But God gave my wife the gift of being able to enjoy the little things in life.

My family and I often like to take trips up to a little town called Solvang, a Danish community in Santa Barbara County, California. I often speak at a Presbyterian church there, and we have several friends in the church. Last Mother's Day, I was working at the computer when an e-mail came through for Deb. It was from one of our friends in Solvang. She said, "Deb, I've been thinking about you for a week. There is a little store here in Solvang that is for sale, and it has all those things that you love: crafts, knickknacks, gifts, collectibles, and even a coffee bar. I was wondering if you would let me put up the money for you to buy that store."

Deb and I laughed because we couldn't imagine how it would work out. But we replied and told her we would think and pray about it.

A few weeks later we made the trip to Solvang to look at the store. It was called Pamela's Country Cupboard, and everything in there looked like the same stuff that had been sitting in my garage for twenty-five years. Of course, Deb fell in love with it, so that summer she became the new owner of Pamela's Country Cupboard in Solvang, California. The only problem? We had to move.

For the first time in twenty-six years of marriage, we were moving for her. We had often had to relocate because of my ministry, but we had never moved anywhere because of Deb. I felt a little weird. However, I knew that God had provided this gift, and he knew how much she would love managing this store. It's also a gift for me, because now I can put all my Harley stuff in the house, since she's moved all her knickknacks to the store.

Paul Little once said, "We see God as a celestial Scrooge who leans down over the balcony of heaven trying to find anyone who's enjoying life and say to them, 'Now, cut it out.'"[1] But that's not who God is. He is a good God, and he loves to give gifts to his children. He loves to see us enjoying the life he has provided.

During his Sermon on the Mount, Jesus said, "Which of you, if his son asks for bread, will give him a stone? Or if he asks for a fish, will give him a snake? If you, then, though you are evil, know how to give good gifts to your children, how much more will your Father in heaven give good gifts to those who ask him" (Matt. 7:9–11).

God is not a tyrant sitting on his throne, giving us a long list of rules and regulations. He is a kind, loving Father who likes to see his children enjoying life. The thoughts we have about God affect the way we perceive his love for us. Do you dwell on what is lovely and admirable—what you appreciate about the Lord? Are your thoughts about God joyful?

Christ came so that we could have life, and have it more abundantly. I believe that God has given us this brief life as a foretaste of what heaven will be like with him—full of joy.

CHAPTER 21

JOY IN CONTENTMENT

I REJOICE GREATLY IN THE LORD THAT AT LAST YOU HAVE RENEWED YOUR CONCERN FOR ME. INDEED, YOU HAVE BEEN CONCERNED, BUT YOU HAD NO OPPORTUNITY TO SHOW IT. I AM NOT SAYING THIS BECAUSE I AM IN NEED, FOR I HAVE LEARNED TO BE CONTENT WHATEVER THE CIRCUMSTANCES. I KNOW WHAT IT IS TO BE IN NEED, AND I KNOW WHAT IT IS TO HAVE PLENTY. I HAVE LEARNED THE SECRET OF BEING CONTENT IN ANY AND EVERY SITUATION, WHETHER WELL FED OR HUNGRY, WHETHER LIVING IN PLENTY OR IN WANT. I CAN DO EVERYTHING THROUGH HIM WHO GIVES ME STRENGTH.

—PHILIPPIANS 4:10–13

Have you ever received money you weren't expecting? Perhaps you were going through a tough time financially, and just when you didn't know how you were going to get through the month, a check showed up from an anonymous benefactor. I love to hear stories of how God has worked through people in this way.

In the context of this passage, Paul is showing appreciation for the Philippians who had provided for him in his need. Other churches had failed him, but they were faithful. At one point they had not been able to support him, but now they had renewed their commitment and Paul was writing to thank them.

Several years ago, I became the pastor at Fair Oaks Church in California. After I had accepted the position, another church, which had supported my evangelistic ministry, wrote a letter explaining that they could no longer contribute financially to Eternity Minded Ministries because I had become a pastor. Their mission statement did not allow them to support pastors.

After I resigned from Fair Oaks in order to spend more time with Eternity Minded Ministries, I called that church; they immediately said they would support me again. They even raised the amount from what they had previously been contributing. I didn't understand all of their reasons for stopping, but I was grateful to have them on board again.

I can relate to Paul's circumstances in this passage because I know how wonderful it feels to have people stand by you in the ministry. Sometimes I don't know how to express my thanks to those who make it possible for me to fulfill my calling to travel and preach the gospel around the world. I couldn't do it without those Christians who faithfully give to our ministry. I imagine that Paul was overwhelmed by the generous spirit of the Philippians and so grateful that they had renewed their support.

Then we come to the part that I find a little harder to relate to. Paul says, "I have learned to be content whatever the circumstances" (v. 11). Paul enjoyed the good life, but he had also learned to enjoy the hard life. He knew what it was to have some wealth; he knew what it was to be in poverty. Paul had experienced the classy restaurants, and he had been without food. He could be happy with the Hyatt Regency or content with a prison cell.

Most of us have been in tough times. Many of us have also enjoyed really great times. Can we say that we were content in the bad times as well as the good?

My sons, Ben and Jordan, are almost grown now, but when they were little our family struggled a lot more with finances than we do now. Christmas was a particularly stressful time, as we wondered how we could afford to buy presents for everyone. June was the month that my wife dreaded the most because in

June there were three birthdays, two anniversaries, Father's Day, and school graduations.

As I reminisced with Jordan the other day, he was surprised to hear that for several years during his early childhood, my mother had supplemented my salary just so we could stay in our home. The cars we had were always broken down, and Jordan had to wear Ben's hand-me-downs. The roof in our house leaked, and any repair that needed to be done was always a huge drain financially.

You may have been in a similar situation at some point, or maybe you are going through something like that right now. To me, it was extremely frustrating not to be able to give my family everything, and I definitely wasn't very content.

So what exactly does Paul mean when he says, "I have learned to be content"? Sometimes the best way to define a term is to explain what it is not.

Contentment versus Contempt

In Proverbs 30:8–9, the writer says to God, "Keep falsehood and lies far from me; give me neither poverty nor riches, but give me only my daily bread. Otherwise, I may have too much and disown you and say, 'Who is the LORD?' Or I may become poor and steal, and so dishonor the name of my God."

Few Christians are truly satisfied with what they have. Instead, they view life with contempt because of what they don't have. Contempt is the act of despising someone or something. For me, I despised my situation in life during those early years of raising kids. I didn't like having to worry about whether or not we would be able to keep our house.

Unfortunately, our society tends to breed a contemptuous outlook on life. Contentment doesn't fuel consumerism. In order to get us to buy more things, advertisers have to make us feel discontent with what we have, what we drive, where we live, and what we look like.

I recently read a great book by Alissa Quart entitled *Branded: The Buying and Selling of Teenagers*. She explains that our society's teens are abused and they don't even know it. Thirty-one million teenagers spend $153 billion a year on stuff: CDs, makeup, electronic gadgets, clothes, cars, etc. Fifty-five percent of all seniors in high school work at least three hours a day to afford all that stuff.[1] No wonder we're envious of those who have more—we're being told that having material possessions is what gives us value.

Some people have great contempt for those who have money. They feel that somehow poverty equals spirituality, and the wealthy are less than holy because they are not giving everything up for God. However, I was rather poor, and I wasn't all that spiritual sometimes. Being poor can also come from laziness or carelessness, and it doesn't necessarily make you better or more spiritual than richer people.

Other people have contempt for God because they have so much money that they think they don't need him.

Moses gave this instruction to the Israelites. "When you have eaten and are satisfied, praise the LORD your God for the good land he has given you" (Deut. 8:10). If you have plenty—and most of us do compared to the rest of the world—then what God desires is for you to praise him and give thanks to him. He doesn't say we can't have nice houses or good food. But when God gives us abundance, we can't forget where the blessings come from.

Contentment versus Stoicism

The stoics of Paul's day were people who believed that they should always be self-sufficient. They could handle any situation because they had it together. The Philippians would have been very familiar with stoic philosophy.

At first we might think Paul is being stoic when he says that he can be content with whatever, but then he tells us the reason why—he trusts Christ for strength. While the stoics weren't dependent on anyone or anything, Paul was depending on Jesus for everything.

Paul is saying, "I've learned to be content, but the only reason I've learned to be content is because Christ is in me. I am dependent upon him." This would not have been an easy thing for Paul to do on his own. Being content isn't something that just happens. Paul said that he *learned* to be content. The secret was Christ. He allowed Paul to be content in all things.

This phrase, "I can do all things through Christ who strengthens me," has been used and abused for a long time in the church. I remember playing football in college and that was our slogan before each game. Paul was probably looking down from heaven and thinking, "Dan, I didn't really write that for this occasion." It is a great thought, but Paul's intent was not to say that Christ will give us strength and power in all things, because some things we want to do may not be in his will.

When it comes to contentment, we can handle any situation because Christ gives us strength. Because we have his priorities, we have a better understanding of what is important in life.

Contentment versus Fatalism

In India, if you are born into a family of farmers, you will become a farmer. If you're born poor, you will stay poor for the rest of your life. In that society, there is no ambition or desire to do better. The Christians in that country thrive because they have the hope of knowing that God has something better than this life planned for them.

God did not tell us to be fatalistic and just take whatever comes into our lives. We are not told to live with what is handed to us and never plan or dream. However, what God does tell us is that we need to commit everything to the Lord.

James says, "Now listen, you who say, 'Today or tomorrow we will go to this or that city, spend a year there, carry on business and make money.' Why, you do not even know what will happen tomorrow. What is your life? You are a mist that appears for a little while and then vanishes. Instead, you ought to say, 'If it is the Lord's will, we will live and do this or that'" (James 4:13–15).

If our sole motivation in life is just to get money, success, power, influence, and all those worldly things, we're going to have a struggle. True contentment doesn't come from having all those things, but from an attitude of satisfaction with what God has given us.

The great theologian Martin Luther said, "Next to faith this is the highest art—to be content with the calling in which God has placed you. I have not learned it yet."[2] Luther struggled with it, and we still struggle with it. We don't just wake up one morning and say, "I'm going to be content." It takes work.

Andrew Murray, a South African missionary, had some great thoughts on contentment. He said, "God has brought me here. It is by his will that I am in this place. He will keep me here in his love.... He will make the trial a blessing, teaching me the lessons he intends for me to learn and working in me the grace he means to bestow. In his good time, he can bring me out again, how and when, he knows. So let me say, 'I am here.'"[3]

Paul later wrote to Timothy, "Godliness with contentment is great gain. For we brought nothing into the world, and we can take nothing out of it" (1 Tim. 6:6–7). Sometimes those who are wealthy fall into this temptation, because they put their confidence in money. Hebrews 13:5 warns, "Keep your lives free from the love of money and be content with what you have, because God has said, 'Never will I leave you; never will I forsake you.'"

I appreciate Paul's honesty in this passage. He knew that he couldn't be content on his own, but that Christ would give him the ability to be always satisfied with what he had.

If you have plenty and you are financially sound, praise God for that and give him the glory. If you're going through a difficult time right now, evaluate your situation and try to determine what God is teaching you through this. Maybe he is humbling you, maybe he is guiding you in another direction, or maybe he is teaching you to trust him.

Rather than trying to find contentment in wealth or status, depend on Christ to strengthen you through every situation, whether in plenty or in want, in good times and in bad.

CHAPTER 22

THE END OF THE JOURNEY

YET IT WAS GOOD OF YOU TO SHARE IN MY TROUBLES. MOREOVER, AS YOU PHILIPPIANS KNOW, IN THE EARLY DAYS OF YOUR ACQUAINTANCE WITH THE GOSPEL, WHEN I SET OUT FROM MACEDONIA, NOT ONE CHURCH SHARED WITH ME IN THE MATTER OF GIVING AND RECEIVING, EXCEPT YOU ONLY; FOR EVEN WHEN I WAS IN THESSALONICA, YOU SENT ME AID AGAIN AND AGAIN WHEN I WAS IN NEED. NOT THAT I AM LOOKING FOR A GIFT, BUT I AM LOOKING FOR WHAT MAY BE CREDITED TO YOUR ACCOUNT. I HAVE RECEIVED FULL PAYMENT AND EVEN MORE; I AM AMPLY SUPPLIED, NOW THAT I HAVE RECEIVED FROM EPAPHRODITUS THE GIFTS YOU SENT. THEY ARE A FRAGRANT OFFERING, AN ACCEPTABLE SACRIFICE, PLEASING TO GOD. AND MY GOD WILL MEET ALL YOUR NEEDS ACCORDING TO HIS GLORIOUS RICHES IN CHRIST JESUS. TO OUR GOD AND FATHER BE GLORY FOR EVER AND EVER. AMEN. GREET ALL THE SAINTS IN CHRIST JESUS. THE BROTHERS WHO ARE WITH ME SEND GREETINGS. ALL THE SAINTS SEND YOU GREETINGS, ESPECIALLY THOSE WHO BELONG TO CAESAR'S HOUSEHOLD. THE GRACE OF THE LORD JESUS CHRIST BE WITH YOUR SPIRIT. AMEN.

—PHILIPPIANS 4:14–23

W e have nearly reached the end of our journey together through Philippians. This church was very special to Paul, and he was concerned with their spiritual growth. He wrote this book of joy for them as an encouragement to walk with the Lord. As he wraps up this letter, Paul has a few thoughts to leave with believers that we don't want to miss.

A Promise Not to Forget

Apparently the Philippians gave Paul quite a generous financial gift. It may not have been large compared to what we think of today, but it was enough to leave the church in need. They had such affection for Paul and his ministry that they gave it all.

Paul wasn't just excited about the gift, as he points out in verse 17, but he was looking at the credit it would be to them and the blessing they would receive. Paul knew that he would not be able to repay such a large gift. It was above and beyond what he had expected. However, he does give them this promise in verse 19: "My God will meet all your needs according to his glorious riches in Christ Jesus."

This is another verse, like Philippians 4:13, which Christians have often taken out of context. We like to say this phrase as a comfort to those who are struggling. It is a very Western way of thinking. We believe that God will meet all our needs no matter what. There is some truth to that, but it is much easier to preach that verse in America than to our brothers and sisters in places like Uganda, Ethiopia, or Sudan, where people are starving to death.

I'm not saying that God doesn't take care of his children. But our American way of thinking allows us to toss that phrase around without stopping to think about its implications.

One thing we have to realize is that we don't really understand exactly what our needs are. We may have a good idea of what we *think* our needs are, but God often has a different opinion. Our society tells us that we need certain things to be happy. Sometimes we might mistake our desires for needs.

In a sense Paul is saying, "I understand that you are in need because of the sacrifice you have made for me. I can't pay you back, but my God will take care of you, and reimburse you for what you have done. His riches are beyond comparison."

Paul knew what the Bible had to say about giving. "A generous man will prosper; he who refreshes others will himself be refreshed" (Prov. 11:25). "He who is kind to the poor lends to the LORD, and he will reward him for what he has done" (Prov. 19:17).

One of my favorite ministry verses was written by Paul. Ephesians 3:20–21 says, "Now to him who is able to do immeasurably more than all we ask or imagine, according to his power that is at work within us, to him be glory in the church and in Christ Jesus throughout all generations, for ever and ever! Amen." In the context of this passage, Paul is talking about the way God gives us spiritual gifts and blessings beyond just what we need physically.

If we want to claim the promise in this verse that God will supply all our needs, we have to realize that God expects something from us. Throughout the Old Testament, we see that God's blessings are tied to his people's obedience: "*If* you do this, *then* I will do this." We have to ask: Am I a selfish person? The church at Philippi was definitely not selfish—they were quite generous in their gift to Paul. Do I give to God and others in proportion to what he has given to me?

Perhaps you have experienced times when you have stepped out in faith and given to God, and then he has taken care of you. Like the woman in Luke 21, maybe you have given right down to your last two coins and trusted God to provide for your needs.

Maybe you haven't yet learned to walk by faith, and you're still holding on to confidence in worldly possessions and wealth. This might be keeping you from fully experiencing the joy of letting God bless you beyond what you can imagine.

The next time you sing a song or read a note that says, "My God shall supply all your needs," think about the context of this verse. Remember that if you want to experience this blessing from God, you can't be living for yourself. You have to be giving sacrificially back to God.

The Hope of Forever

Paul concludes this letter in a similar way as he does with his other epistles—with a doxology. "To our God and Father be glory for ever and ever. Amen" (v. 20). Here Paul is practicing what he preached earlier in the chapter. He gives the glory and praise to God for his blessings, acknowledging that everything he has comes from God.

A young woman came up to me one Sunday after I finished preaching to share with me her story of thankfulness. Lisa's father had called one day and said that he needed to come over and talk. Lisa was nervous, and she sent up a quick prayer to God for help to say the right things.

When he arrived, he was already crying. He told her that he was so thankful for everything he had—for his family, his home, his job—and he had come to the realization that it could only be from God. He wanted to thank the Lord, but he didn't know how. Lisa was able to spend some time praying with him and thanking God for his blessings.

After that night, both her parents started attending church and accepted Christ. The part that amazed her, Lisa said, was that it would have been really easy for her dad to say, "It was my own doing." He was a fairly successful person, but he knew deep down inside that he couldn't take credit for all the blessings in his life.

Lisa's dad passed away several years ago, but she told me that she gives thanks every day to God for saving him. Now he is able to stand personally before God and say thank you.

In his commentary on Philippians, Gordon Fee writes, "When one thinks of the riches of God lavished upon us in Christ Jesus, what else is there to do but to praise and worship forever and ever?"[1] Lisa's father is experiencing that now, praising God forever and ever.

Paul had the incredible ability to see things from an eternal perspective, and he was able to interpret everything in the light of eternity. Not only did he realize that everything on this earth came from God, but he also understood how much more we will have when we get to heaven.

I want my life to be a doxology, an expression of praise to God, not just forever and ever in the future but forever and ever starting right now. In light of how richly we have been blessed, how can we not want to thank God for what he has done?

Sadhu Sundar Singh, a prominent Christian from India who lived in the early twentieth century, wrote these words about fellowship with God. "Some people become tired at the end of ten minutes or a half hour of prayer. What will they do when they have to spend eternity in the presence of God? We must begin the habit here and become used to being with God."[2]

Is God huge to you? And are you comfortable being with God? Remember, we're going to be with him forever and ever. If you're not comfortable with him today, what makes you think you're going to be comfortable with him down the road a little bit?

I once had dinner with a research doctor at a theological conference in Sacramento. He shared with me that he had grown up in a legalistic Christian home and had soon realized that it did not bring him satisfaction. So he began to research, reading books, looking at various denominations, and gleaning as much information as possible. Amazed, I asked him, "And what did you discover in all this reading and research?"

He smiled and said, "The one thing I know is, after reading and researching tirelessly for the last twelve years, I know less about God now than I did before, but I love him so much more." That is so true! The more you study, the more you realize what you don't know, but the closer you grow in your relationship with God, if you are truly seeking to know his character more intimately.

Help for the Journey

Finally, Paul says, "The grace of the Lord Jesus Christ be with your spirit." Your spirit is a part of you that you don't want to ignore. In 1 Thessalonians 5:23, Paul writes, "May God himself, the God of peace, sanctify you through and through. May your whole spirit, soul and body be kept blameless at the coming of our Lord Jesus Christ."

Spirit, soul, and body. We tend to look at those three things in reverse order. We want to take care of our bodies first, and we'll usually take care of our souls, and then maybe we'll take care of our spirits.

In our culture, we are told that our first priority should be us—our bodies. We need the trendiest clothes or the nicest haircut or the best food. Sometimes we are encouraged to take care of our souls—our personality and emotions. We have lots of resources like recovery groups and self-help books to assist us in taking care of our souls.

But what about the spirit? What about that part that enables us to perceive the divine, to connect with spiritual things? It is what allows us to communicate with God. God has given us this gift of a spirit in order that we may understand the things we can't see with our eyes or comprehend with our mind or intellect.

Helen Keller, who was blind and deaf, said, "The best and most beautiful things in the world cannot be seen or even touched. They must be felt with the heart."[3] In your spirit, do you feel God? Do you sense his Spirit in your life? That was the desire that Paul had for the church that he loved.

Information and doctrine are important, but in the end he says, "My brothers and sisters, those whom I love, I pray that your spirit may be connected to Christ, and that you may know him intimately."

Is your experience with God real? Is the Holy Spirit's ministry in your life real? We go to the doctors and get checkups to evaluate our physical bodies. But do we evaluate our spirits?

The Bible is our map, and our destination is walking in the Spirit, knowing God more closely each day. My prayer for you is that through this study in Philippians, you have grown in joy and fellowship with the living God. May your joy continue to increase as you travel this journey of life, and as you understand what a great God we serve!

READERS' GUIDE
FOR PERSONAL REFLECTION OR GROUP STUDY

Chapter 1

1. "Despite his troubles, and Paul certainly had plenty of them, he was able to say, 'My joy knows no bounds.'" Do you have joy during hardships? Why or why not?

2. "But these material difficulties and tempests in your soul, how can they compare to the joy of knowing Jesus?" What do you allow to crowd out the joy of knowing Jesus in your life?

3. "By giving this blessing, Paul reminds the Philippian church of the result of grace in a believer's life: peace." Do you have inner peace? Peace with God? Peace with your Christian community? If not, why do you think this is? Is grace lacking in your life?

4. "We can safely assume that Paul had an awesome prayer life. One of the reasons for that, I believe, is that he allowed his prayers to be guided by the Holy Spirit." How do you know that your prayers are guided by the Holy Spirit?

5. "As you go through the week and people come to your mind, even if you don't know what's going on in their lives, consider that the Lord may be prompting you to give someone a phone call, or write a note of encouragement, or just stop and pray for someone." Who has been on your mind lately? How are you going to respond to the Lord's promptings?

Chapter 2

1. "Somehow in our experience, unfortunately sometimes even in church, we get it into our heads that God is really not for us." Have you ever felt this way? How did you respond to your feelings?

2. "We look at people and oftentimes determine whether or not we love them by their outward appearance." What are the consequences of such selective love?

3. "Growing love involves sacrificing time, money, and comfort in order to reach out to those who need to hear our good news." Think of three practical ways that you can love your "neighbor." Make a plan to carry through with those things this week.

4. "Do you truly experience God, or do you just have a lot of book learning?" How do you know that your knowledge is experiential knowledge?

5. "Our goal is to be able to discern what is right. Sometimes that might mean saying 'no' to something that is good."

Have you said "yes" to "good" commitments that keep you from knowing God better as you spend time with him?

Chapter 3

1. "Paul lived in a different realm that we, too, can live in. He had a different worldview—not of his world, but God's world." How does viewing life through God's worldview change your perspective on your current situation and challenges?

2. "Our 'advances' have stolen away our true belief in the supernatural, reducing life to this material world that we live in—what we can taste, what we can see, what we can touch, what we can smell." How could having a material worldview prevent you from understanding God's purposes in your life?

3. Read Ephesians 6. How is your struggle against the powers and forces of evil rather than "flesh and blood"?

4. "Paul took advantage of his environment to share the message of Christ." What situations or experiences seem to enable you to more easily share the gospel? What situations or experiences are obstacles for you in sharing the gospel? How are you moving past these obstacles?

5. "I pray that we have that kind of courage and boldness to seize every opportunity to advance the gospel, as Paul did." Whom do you know who needs to hear the gospel? Plan a time to talk to that person about what Jesus has done in your life.

Chapter 4

1. "Worship. Grow. Tell. That's the three-fold mission of the church." How do you live out the three-fold mission?

2. "Maybe it's fear, maybe it's laziness—but we often have a hard time stepping out of our comfort zone and bringing the good news of the gospel to our friends and family." What keeps you from sharing your faith? What can you do to overcome this obstacle?

3. "Paul repeatedly urged others to take courage—because of God's sure promises and because of the need for action." What is the source of your courage?

4. "There's no need to fear. The worst thing that could happen to you and me is nothing compared to the goodness waiting for us in God's presence." How do you respond to troubling circumstances? Is that how God wants you to respond?

5. "The circumstances may not have happened the way we planned, but they were never out of God's control, and he worked everything out for his glory." Read Romans 8:28. How has God worked everything out in a distressing circumstance in your life?

Chapter 5

1. "Paul's confidence was not in himself—it was in the Lord." Who—or what—is your confidence really in? How do you know?

2. "One of the ministries of the Holy Spirit is to make us aware that someone else needs prayer." Describe a time that God prompted you to pray for someone else.

3. "So much of what we say we believe has yet to be tested." What is the "benefit" of testing what we believe? When has this happened to you?

4. "Timid creatures and self-absorbed individuals become different when the Spirit transforms their lives. He gives us that courage, that power to change." How has the Holy Spirit transformed your life?

5. "'Whether I'm alive on planet earth or whether I die, I want my life to be used as a telescope to bring Christ closer to people.' That was [Paul's] goal. That was his driving passion." What are your goals for your life and death?

Chapter 6

1. "Paul certainly enjoyed life, but he had a bigger picture. He had joy in his present circumstances, and even more joy in his future circumstances." In what ways does the promise of heaven give you joy today?

2. "We can enjoy Christ right now." How do you enjoy Christ right now?

3. "In Paul's heart he knew the ultimate joy was to be with the Lord." Does your enjoyment of Christ now make you long for heaven?

4. "It doesn't matter what your qualifications are. Your life is meaningful because you're motivated out of love and you serve out of love." How does this statement encourage you?

5. "Someone once said to me, 'There are two ways to walk into a room. You can walk into the room and say, "Here I am." Or you can walk into the room and say, "There you are."'" What is your attitude toward the people around you? Here I am? Or there you are?

Chapter 7

1. "Unity does not come from without, but from within." What does this mean for church unity?

2. "In 1 Corinthians 12, Paul explains that we are all members of one body." Read 1 Corinthians 12. As a member of the body of Christ, how important are your contributions of love and service?

3. "Have you had a time like that in your life, that 'bitterness of soul,' when everything looks dark all around you?" During that time, what was your greatest source of comfort? Did you feel comforted by God?

4. "The only problem is, if you don't work through it with Jesus, when you're done with the pills, the problem is still there. He is still trying to work. He is still trying to deal with you, and often we prolong the situation." Describe a time when you prolonged healing by pursuing your own "cure."

5. "When you're in pain—emotional or physical—you want somebody who's tender and compassionate." How is God a tender and compassionate comforter to you now?

Chapter 8

1. "People don't want to see themselves in the light of their own arrogance or pride." In what areas of your life do you see arrogance or pride?

2. "Paul lifts up the word *humility*. Christians should be very familiar with this word." Why should the idea of submission and humility be less offensive to Christians?

3. "Robert Schuller has said, 'The easiest job in the world for God is to humble a human being.'" How does your pride stand between you and God?

4. "Some people are filled with pride and arrogance.... Then there is the opposite extreme, in which an individual despises himself. He literally abhors himself. That, too, is a sin of a different kind." What is the problem with hating yourself? What does Ephesians 2:4–5 say is the reason for God giving us salvation? Does this quality match self-hatred?

5. "Real humility is displayed by the person who is not consumed with himself or herself, but is consumed with who God is and what he has asked us to do for other people." Does real humility characterize your life? If not, what can you do to become humble?

6. "Humility brings freedom. As long as we walk around like we've got it all together, like we have no weaknesses, we're just deceiving ourselves." Do you feel bound by your need to appear to have it "together"? How might humility bring you freedom?

Chapter 9

1. "We say we want to be like Jesus, but the question we each must ask is Do we really?" Do you really want to be like Jesus? Why?

2. "If we truly want to be like Jesus, we must address these questions: Where do we submit? Does our submission show up in our relationships, at church, with people at work, and within our family?" Where do you show Christlike submission?

3. "Jesus washed his disciples' feet like a common house slave. This is the same attitude that we are supposed to have as men and women who want to be like Christ." Read John 13:1–17. What does verse 15 tell us? How are you obeying Jesus' command?

4. "God sometimes calls us to do something that is a little outside our comfort zone. That's when we truly have to submit and we have to serve." What could God be calling you to do that is outside of your comfort zone?

5. "We say, 'I want to be like Jesus,' yet the word *sacrifice* is something we shy away from. Sacrifice means that there is

going to be a price to pay and pain will be involved." What is your attitude about sacrifice like? Is it like Christ's?

Chapter 10

1. "Every created being will bow down before the Lord Jesus Christ." How does this make you feel? Should you make changes in your life today in light of this?

2. "Some might hear the truth but never grasp it. They never submit to that truth." Read Matthew 13:1–23. What was Jesus teaching through this parable?

3. "How will it be for those who have lived their life with no responsibility and no care about what God thinks?" How does the knowledge that your life will be examined influence your choices and actions?

4. "To become a follower of Jesus, three things have to be working together: my emotions, my mind, and my will that says, 'Lord, I want to follow you.'" How are these three things working together in your life?

5. "Jesus makes it very clear that the true mark of Christianity, the true mark of devotion to him, is one who is producing the fruit of the Spirit." Read Galatians 5:22–26. Is the fruit of the Spirit evident in your life?

Chapter 11

1. "The light of Christ should be reflected in our lives from the moment we become Christians." When did you become a Christian? Reflect on the change that has occurred in you since then.

2. "C. S. Lewis has said that those who do the most for this world are the ones who think the most about the next. If I am a shining light, how committed am I to the next world—to eternity?" How does the thought of eternity impact your daily living?

3. "I value life above anything else. However, God does not see it that way. He sees our spirits as more important than our bodies." What causes you to believe that this is true?

4. "Grumbling, fighting, and complaining distract us from the task. They sidetrack us from what we should be doing." Do you find yourself commenting on the negative rather than enjoying the positive side of things? Does this make you more or less effective? How?

5. "Our ministry is to hold forth the word of life, and shine as bright stars in a dark world." How do you do this? How do you want to do this?

Chapter 12

1. "But they knew of Timothy's proven character. It wasn't just about personality. In America we get really attached to that. If we like a person's personality, we'll hang around him or

her; otherwise, we move on to the next person." How is character different than personality?

2. "There are also difficulties in this world. There are difficulties in this Christian life." Read John 16:33. What response was Jesus looking for?

3. "What kind of a friend are you? When people you call friends go through difficult times, do you walk out or walk in?" What do your friendships reveal about your heart attitudes?

4. "Even at church, we will talk among other believers about the weather, our kids, or our Sunday afternoon plans, but we rarely ask the tough questions." Do you talk to other Christians differently than you talk to unbelievers? How?

Chapter 13

1. "Too often I'm afraid we study the Bible to gather details and create a rulebook to follow. We miss the emotion of what the author wants to communicate to us." How do you study the Bible? Do you think that is the way God desires for you to view his Word?

2. "Life does not always go as we have planned. We will often go through disappointments." What disappointments are you going through now? Do you believe that God is working through them?

3. "I love how the Lord lets us be honest with our emotions. Scripture shows that the disciples were obviously angry. One of the great things about being a Christian is that you can tell the Lord exactly how you feel." Read Mark 4:35–41. What did the disciples say to Jesus? What was their final thought about him?

4. "If you didn't have [difficulties] this week, you may have them next week.... When things are going well, it's good to celebrate. The difficulties and the good times are all part of God's plan." How do you celebrate and thank God for the good times and the blessings?

5. "We are often disappointed by other people's weaknesses. We tend to judge them based on our strengths, and we feel like we need to fix them." How do you do this? What would happen if you "judged" people based on their strengths?

Chapter 14

1. "It's interesting that so many times our discipleship is focused on those who've known the Lord a long time, instead of providing new Christians with strong fellowship groups. They are often the ones who most need encouragement and teaching." If you have been a Christian for a while, consider discipling a newer Christian. How might you bring encouragement and teaching to them?

2. "But [Paul] remembered Jesus' teaching—the real issue is in the heart, not the outward appearance." Read 1 Samuel 16:1–13. What is the context for verse 7? What was Samuel looking for? What was God looking for?

3. "People have always said, 'You should wear your best to church because it's God house and you need to show reverence for him.' There is some truth to that, but I believe that Jesus is more concerned with the heart." How important is our physical appearance to God, according to 1 Samuel 16:7? Is there anytime that our physical appearance reflects our heart?

4. "How are you at living in the Spirit?" Do you listen to the Holy Spirit? How is this seen in your life?

5. "We can boast about Jesus and what he has done for us." What has Jesus done for you? Don't be ashamed to boast about it today!

6. "Building a relationship with God takes time in worship and prayer. Yet that is what Christ is calling us to—a relationship where we truly experience him." Are you building a relationship with God? If not, begin by praying and reading his Word to you—the Bible.

Chapter 15

1. "All the notoriety, all the accolades, and all his accomplishments were present gains that were nothing when compared to knowing Christ. He considered them rubbish—literally 'garbage.'" Is this the way that you view your accomplishments and credentials?

2. "G. K. Chesterton wrote, 'Let your religion be less of a theory and more of a love affair.'" Is your religion a theory or a love affair? What would the people who know you best say?

3. "Because we have the experience of this relationship, we can trust Jesus." How does knowing Jesus—rather than knowing about Jesus—enable us to trust him?

4. "Religion has no power to save or transform. Real power comes from a relationship with Jesus, who gives us the power to change and who transforms us to glorify him." What or who has the power to transform you? How do you know?

5. "In verse 10, Paul prays to know Christ and the power of his resurrection." Read Philippians 3:10. How is the resurrection related to our present lives two thousand years later?

6. "We hate suffering in America. In our mindset, we do everything we can to avoid suffering. The most horrible thing we can think about is death." In what ways is this true for you? What is the Christian's response to suffering and death?

Chapter 16

1. "We tend to struggle with being totally open and honest.... [We] stay guarded.... Instead, it would be so much better if we could have the transparency that Paul uses." How would transparency change your church community? What steps can you begin to take in order to be open and honest?

2. "Some Christians are carrying around a spiritual ball and chain, unable to run because they have resentment or bitterness tucked away inside of them." Read Philippians 3:12–14. Are you running the race the way Paul described

it—with perseverance and determination? Or do you have a spiritual ball and chain that is slowing you down?

3. "Maybe you have experienced that feeling of being laden with guilt, feeling like the Lord is so far away. We let some sin creep into our lives and then Jesus feels like a stranger." What sin is coming between you and Jesus? Repent and turn back to him; you'll find that he is right there!

4. "Most of us naturally have goals in our lives, whether it's to get wealthy, or to become successful in business, or to raise wonderful children. But how often do we set spiritual goals?" Write down three to five spiritual goals, such as, "Learn how to share the gospel clearly and correctly."

5. "C. S. Lewis said, 'Aim at heaven and you will get earth thrown in. Aim at earth and you get neither.'" Where is your aim? Do your money, time, thoughts, and actions agree with your answer?

Chapter 17

1. "[They] set their minds on earthly things. In contrast, Paul was focusing on the future and his heavenly prize." Read 1 John 2:15–17. Where is your mind and focus set?

2. "If I only miss church two Sundays a year, or pray a certain amount of time each day, will that give me a balanced Christian life? Of course not. Paul is talking about right motives, priorities, and goals." What does a "balanced Christian life" look like?

3. "But when we stop for a moment and meditate and reflect on who God is, our lives fall into balance. We let him in, and he brings our lives back to order." Describe a time when you saw this in your own life. What things keep you from reflecting on God today?

4. "The reason we need to be balanced, Paul explains, is that we are waiting for Jesus' return. That thought should have a major impact on our lives." How often do you think of Jesus' return? How does that thought influence your decisions?

5. "Are you living a balanced Christian life right now? If Jesus came back today, would you be ashamed to stand before him because you have either been legalistic or lazy in your relationship with him?" Which "side" do you tend to be on? What should you do to bring your life into balance?

Chapter 18

1. "Unfortunately, conflict sometimes destroys our unity, especially in the local church." Read John 17:20–26. What is Jesus' desire for his church? How do we compare today?

2. "Running away from conflict will not resolve it. We need to realize that conflict is part of life—whether you see it in the office, at home, or at a Bible study." How does standing firm in the Lord (v. 1) keep you from running away from conflict?

3. "The health of a church, just like the health of a business organization, can rise and fall on one conflict that is allowed to grow instead of being dealt with." Read Matthew

12:25. Identify a conflict in your life. What can you do to promote unity in that situation?

4. "If you are on the other side of the situation, and have been the one wronged by another Christian, Jesus says, 'If your brother sins against you, go and show him his fault, just between the two of you. If he listens to you, you have won your brother over' (Matt. 18:15). Later in the passage, Jesus lays out the rest of the plan if the person does not repent." Read Matthew 18:15–20. What are Jesus' instructions when someone wrongs you?

5. "Even though they may say, 'Yes, I forgive you,' to the other person, they still harbor hard feelings, and they still talk among their friends—their secondaries—about how they have been hurt." Is this real forgiveness? If not, what is?

Chapter 19

1. "We have all had situations in our lives when we have found it difficult to be joyful. When we experience disappointment, when people hurt us, or when our lives are full of trials or grief, we don't really feel like rejoicing." Why is it still important to rejoice during hard times?

2. "First, complaining is a particularly serious offense in light of how we have been so greatly blessed—especially when we complain about trivial things." How is complaining a serious offense in light of God's blessings to us?

3. "Joy is the mark of the Holy Spirit in our lives…. Joy is not based on temperament, personality, or feelings, but on how

we let the indwelling Holy Spirit control our lives." Do you have joy? What does that reveal about the condition of your heart before God?

4. "Jesus was the ultimate example of [gentleness]." Read 1 Peter 2:23 and Isaiah 53. How was Jesus gentle? How should we be gentle?

5. "How do we stop worrying? Paul's answer is by prayer. He doesn't say, 'read your Bible,' or 'read a book about prayer.' We have to really commune with the living God." What is worrying you right now? Take it to God in prayer.

6. "This peace is a gift that God gives when we have a wor-shipping heart, when we have a heart that is dedicated to him, and when we ask him for guidance, healing, and strength. It stems from a regular prayer life in which we bring our will in line with God's perfect plan." Do you have God's peace "which transcends all understanding"?

Chapter 20

1. "This peace he talks about will guard our hearts and our minds, but we have a responsibility to control what we allow our thoughts to dwell on." Do you have control over your thought life? How do you know?

2. "Jesus taught his disciples that sin begins in the mind. James tells us that sin can start out as a small desire—a mere thought. Our thoughts reveal who we really are." Read Matthew 5:21–30 and James 1:13–15. What do your thoughts say about you?

3. "I believe that part of what Paul is saying here is that we can enjoy our culture and still be a strong follower of Jesus." Which parts of our culture are "lovely"? Do you enjoy these as Jesus enjoyed the "lovely" aspects of his culture?

4. "We can enjoy our culture and the life we have, but we must be careful not to be captivated by the things of this world." What is the difference between enjoying and being captivated?

5. "The thoughts we have about God affect the way we perceive his love for us. Do you dwell on what is lovely and admirable—what you appreciate about the Lord? Are your thoughts about God joyful?" Read Matthew 7:9–11. How does our heavenly Father treat us? Thank God right now for all that he has done for you.

Chapter 21

1. "Most of us have been in tough times. Many of us have also enjoyed really great times." Can you say along with Paul, "I have learned to be content whatever the circumstances"?

2. "So what exactly does Paul mean when he says, 'I have learned to be content'?" Read Proverbs 30:8–9. What is contentment?

3. "Some people have great contempt for those who have money. They feel that somehow poverty equals spirituality, and the wealthy are less than holy because they are not giving everything up for God." How do you know that poverty does not equal spirituality? Can you think of any examples?

4. "If you have plenty—and most of us do compared to the rest of the world—then what God desires is for you to praise him and give thanks to him. He doesn't say we can't have nice houses or good food. But when God gives us abundance, we can't forget where the blessings come from." Do you have "plenty"? Do you praise God for his blessings?

5. "Being content isn't something that just happens. Paul said that he *learned* to be content. The secret was Christ." How does Christ teach you to be content? How does Christ make a difference in our contentment?

Chapter 22

1. "We believe that God will meet all our needs no matter what. There is some truth to that, but it is much easier to preach that verse in America than to our brothers and sisters in places like Uganda, Ethiopia, or Sudan, where people are starving to death." What is Philippians 4:19 really saying? What is the context?

2. "If we want to claim the promise in this verse that God will supply all our needs, we have to realize that God expects something from us. Throughout the Old Testament, we see that God's blessings are tied to his people's obedience: '*If* you do this, *then* I will do this.'" Read Deuteronomy 28:1–6, 15–19. These verses were given to the Israelites before they entered the Promised Land. What do they tell us about God's expectations for us?

3. "Gordan Fee writes, 'When one thinks of the riches of God lavished upon us in Christ Jesus, what else is there to do but

to praise and worship forever and ever?'" Make a list of the blessings God has given you. Spend time praising God for everything on your list.

4. "I want my life to be a doxology, an expression of praise to God, not just forever and ever in the future but forever and ever starting right now." How can you do this in your own life?

5. "Information and doctrine are important, but in the end he says, 'My brothers and sisters, those whom I love, I pray that your spirit may be connected to Christ, and that you may know him intimately.'" Do you take care of your spirit? How so?

NOTES

Chapter 1
1. The Voice of the Martyrs, *Extreme Devotion* (Nashville: W Publishing Group, 2001), 218.
2. Howard Taylor, *J. Hudson Taylor: God's Man in China* (Chicago: Moody Press, 1981), 6.

Chapter 2
1. Mike Yaconelli, *Messy Spirituality* (Grand Rapids: Zondervan, 2002), 89.

Chapter 4
1. David Sanford, "Ross' Story," © 2005, used by permission.
2. Oswald Chambers, *My Utmost for His Highest* "March 15th" (New York: Dodd, Mead & Company, 1935).

Chapter 8
1. Robert H. Schuller, *Self-Esteem: The New Reformation* (Nashville: W Publishing Group, 1982), 57.
2. John Wesley, "The Witness of the Spirit," ed., Thomas Jackson, Sermon 10, Part II, pt. 6, 1872, http://wesley.nnu.edu/john%5Fwesley/sermons/010.htm.
3. Jim Bakker, *I Was Wrong* (Nashville: Thomas Nelson Publishers, 1996), 609–610.
4. Mark Water, ed., *The New Encyclopedia of Christian Quotations* (Grand Rapids: Baker Books, 2000), 826.

Chapter 10
1. Water, *Christian Quotations*, 466.
2. Charles Spurgeon, *The Treasury of David* (Grand Rapids: Kregel, 2004), 358.

Chapter 11
1. "Livermore's Centennial Light," http://www.centennialbulb.org/facts.htm, June 3, 2005.
2. C. S. Lewis, quoted at www.quotedb.com/quotes/2494.
3. Philip Yancey, "Forgetting God," *Christianity Today*, September 2004, 104.
4. Martin Luther King Jr., quoted in Philip Yancey, "The Colonizers" *Christianity Today*, January 2004, 80.

Chapter 12
1. Water, *Christian Quotations*, 385.
2. Ibid.

Chapter 13
1. Water, *Christian Quotations*, 278.

Chapter 14
1. Water, *Christian Quotations*, 975.

Chapter 15
1. "Gilbert K. Chesterson Quotes," http://brainyquotes.com/quotes/quotes/g/gilbertkc107505.html, June 3, 2005.
2. Tertullian, *De testimonio animae*, trans., S. Thelwall, chapter 1, 1869, http://www.tertullian.net/anf/anf03/anf03-20.htm.

Chapter 16
1. "C. S. Lewis Quotes," http://www.brainyquote.com/quotes/quotes/c/cslewis11535 2.html, June 3, 2005.

Chapter 17
1. A. W. Tozer, *The Root of the Righteous* (Harrisburg, PA: Christian Publications, 1986), 156.

Chapter 18
1. Water, *Christian Quotations*, 1085.
2. Ibid.

Chapter 19
1. Jeremiah Burroughs, *The Rare Jewel of Christian Contentment* (Lafayette, IN: Sovereign Grace Publishers, 2001).
2. Water, *Christian Quotations*, 449.
3. Ibid.

Chapter 20
1. Paul Little, *Know Why You Believe* (Downers Grove, IL: InterVarsity Press, 2000), 33–34.

Chapter 21
1. Alissa Quart, *Branded: The Buying and Selling of Teenagers* (New York: Basic Books, 2004), 15.
2. Water, *Christian Quotations,* 224.
3. Ibid.

Chapter 22
1. Gordon D. Fee, *Paul's Letter to the Philippians* (Grand Rapids: Eerdmans, 1995), 455.
2. Water, *Christian Quotations,* 369.
3. Ibid., 366.

ABOUT THE AUTHOR AND ETERNITY MINDED MINISTRIES

Over the past two decades, across America and in nearly forty countries, Daniel Owens has proclaimed the Gospel of Jesus Christ and has communicated the need for personal renewal to hundreds of thousands of people.

Christianity Today profiled Dan Owens as one of fifty "Up and Comers"—one of "the many faithful disciples God has raised up to lead the church into the new millennium." This recognition came because of his unique ability to adapt his contemporary messages to impact any audience. The British publication *Evangelism Today* says, "Dan Owens has a winsome way with words, and a smile that makes it possible to say almost anything without giving offense."

Dan Owens is also the author of *Sharing Christ When You Feel You Can't* (Crossway), *In God We Trust ... But Only As a Last Resort* (Crossway), and *A Faith That Is Real* (Victor, Cook Communications, 2006). Dan has helped train thousands of Christians to build bridges to the unchurched world. He is an engaging speaker who is passionate about communicating the need for personal renewal.

Before he founded Eternity Minded Ministries, Dan Owens served with the Luis Palau Evangelistic Association as Director of Training and an Associate Evangelist for eleven years.

Dan Owens is a graduate of Christian Heritage College (San Diego, California) and Multnomah Seminary (Portland, Oregon).

An approved Staley lecturer for colleges and universities, Dan has been a featured speaker at Alive Festival, Creation Festival, Spirit Fest Midwest, and other youth events across the country and around the world.

Whether speaking to thousands of teenagers at a rally, college students at a university, adults at a missions conference, or families at a festival, Dan Owens is at home in front of people. Listening to this fun, dynamic, and compelling speaker, audiences are moved to consider *eternity*!

Before crusade and festival meetings, Dan Owens and his associates train Christians in friendship evangelism, counseling, and follow-up. This training increases the effectiveness of the evangelistic outreach and equips church members for ongoing evangelism long after the crusade or festival ends.

Dan and his wife, Deb, have been married for more than twenty-five years. They have three sons: Ben (born in 1982), Jordan (born in 1985), and Taylor (born in 1996).

For more information contact:
Eternity Minded Ministries
P.O. Box 502101
San Diego, California 92150
(858) 675-9477
dan@eternityminded.org
www.eternityminded.org

FREE ONLINE RESOURCES

Be sure to log on to www.eternityminded.org today to write a brief letter to Daniel Owens. He would love to hear how this book has helped you enjoy a more authentic faith!

On the www.eternityminded.org Web site, you will discover a treasure chest of free ministry resources and Eternity Minded Ministries updates. You can also sign up for Dan Owens' free ministry newsletter so you can pray for his ministry, keep in touch, and someday perhaps ask Dan to speak at your church or conference.

Online you can find out if Dan Owens will be speaking in your area and listen to some of his most popular messages and radio programs. You can also request a free CD.

Check it out today!

Additional copies of *A Joy That Is Real*
are available wherever good books are sold.

If you have enjoyed this book, or if it has had
an impact on your life,
we would like to hear from you.

Please contact us at:

VICTOR BOOKS
Cook Communications Ministries, Dept. 201
4050 Lee Vance View
Colorado Springs, CO 80918

Or visit our Web site:
www.cookministries.com

The Bible Teacher's Teacher